D0463589

KAREN!
KAREN!

KAREN! KAREN!

One woman's
response to the
whispers of God

*by Karen
Burton
Mains*

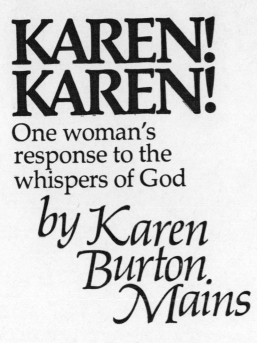

Tyndale House
Publishers, Inc.
Wheaton, Illinois

All Scripture quotes are
from the Revised Standard
Version unless otherwise
indicated.

Library of Congress
Catalog Card Number
78-64675.
ISBN 0-8423-2025-3,
paper.
Copyright © 1979 by
Karen Burton Mains,
Wheaton, Illinois. All
rights reserved.
First printing, January 1979.
Printed in the United
States of America.

To D A V I D
In whom the Word of God
is incarnated
richly . .

CONTENTS

PROLOGUE

In the beginning was the Word
And the Word was with God,
And the Word was God.

"And God said to Noah..."
A rain and cloud-filled word.
"Then the Lord said to Moses..."
A burning-bush and mountain-fire word.
"Then the Lord said to Joshua..."
"And the angel of the Lord appeared to Gideon..."
"And the Spirit of the Lord
came mightily upon Samson."

"And the Lord came and stood forth,
calling as at other times,
'Samuel; Samuel!' "

"The word of the Lord came to Nathan..."
"At Gibeon the Lord appeared to Solomon
In a dream by night."

"And the word of the Lord came to Jehu..."
And to Elijah the Tishbite
came the still small voice-word.

To Job came the whirlwind-word.
And Isaiah saw the Lord
"sitting upon a throne,
high and lifted up;
and his train filled the Temple."
And he heard the voice of the Lord saying,
"Whom shall I send, and who will go for us?"

The word of the Lord came
to Jeremiah and Ezekiel...
Daniel heard a man's voice
between the banks of the Ulai.

The word of the Lord came
to Hosea and to Joel and to Amos.
To Jonah came the whale-word,
"Arise, go to Nineveh,
that great city,
and cry against it..."

Still came on the prophet word,
to Micah and Nahum,
to Habakkuk and Zephaniah,
to Haggai,
to Zechariah,
to Malachi.

Till finally,
the Word became flesh,
and dwelt among us,
full of grace and truth.

"KAREN! KAREN!"

"Karen! Karen!"

My mother's voice called. She had left me in charge of house and younger sister and brother and with a list of chores while she made a quick dash to go purchase groceries. As the eldest child, eleven years old, many home responsibilities had fallen my way.

"Karen!" she called again. "I have something for you!"

I had spent that morning cleaning my summer room. It was rented to college students for the school term, then became my very own for three lovely months. I imagine the football players who lived there during winter, spring, and fall were mildly tolerant of the feminine spreads and matching curtains sprinkled with tiny blue apples, striped with white, and festooned with ruffles. The young men may have possessed the room the majority of the seasons, but I occupied it all year with my decorating taste.

The room felt like a cottage with its double row of windows marching along two walls. Hinged at the top like those of a summer cabin, they swung inward and latched to hooks on the ceiling. A corner room, it caught the east and south sunshine which scattered leafy shadows through the tree of heaven clambering outside, onto the floor and two desks (for two students) and mirrors.

Overlooking the backyard with its branched box elder tree

shading swing and sandpile and buggy inhabitants, it smelled of fresh-mown grass. Peonies bordered the vegetable garden with its rows of beans and lettuce. Currant bushes yielded their beaded fruits, and a wild fat grapevine coiled, sturdy enough to bear the climbing, shrieking adventures of children.

This day, in that room, I had been absorbed with God. *Was I really his child?* A frightening hole gaped in my soul. Perhaps I didn't belong to him, but only *thought* that I did. How could a person know for certain? How could a girl-child of eleven know beyond doubt? What if I was really a heathen? The awful possibilities bumped about within me, knocking against each other loudly.

"Lord," I prayed simply, not worrying about weighty theological questions (they were, fortunately, beyond me). "Lord, if I'm really your child, help me to be a good girl today." I had no idea, nor did I consider, how I would know if indeed I had been "a good girl today."

The room was almost shining clean when I heard my mother calling my name. Running downstairs, I found her bustling in the kitchen which my father had so painstakingly remodeled. The lovely cabinet he had built (and which we children had helped to build by sitting as weights on the end of whatever board he happened to be sawing) hung above the eating table, which was piled with brown paper packages.

"Oh, there you are." Mother smiled. "I have something for you." From one of the sacks she drew a small cylinder of stick cologne and handed it to me.

"This is for you," she explained. "This is because you have been such a good girl."

The world stood still as it often does when we know God is bending near. I took the jar of scent, my first, and ran back to the summer room with its blue apples marching in proper order down freshly made beds, and pondered this startling answer to prayer which had just come to me.

In ecclesiastical jargon, I was assured of my salvation. Since the age of eleven, I have never once doubted that I belonged to God. Often I've been amazed at his persistence in continuing to bother with me, but the fact of our kinship was permanently sealed on that summer day.

Strangely for a child, I never used that cologne. It sat in my cupboard for years. I suppose it had become a symbol of the sacred. It was as granite to me—permanent as any monument ever erected in memoriam. It was my pillar of stones piled by the wayside, my Ebenezer raised, my flying standard.

"And the Word of the Lord came unto the child, Karen . . ."

Of the many spiritual crises I have experienced in my life, this was undoubtedly the first. I wondered if I belonged to God. The supernatural intervened and I recognized it. Since then I have learned that the Word has the potential of always coming, in the most amazing variety of ways—some humorous, some wrenching. By offering himself at this strategic moment of my need, God taught me a truth far beyond the matter of assurance. I became convinced of his reality. I knew that he was.

Daniel 11:32 declares that they "that do know their God shall . . . do exploits." Yet, how do we—mundane, ordinary, everyday human beings come to know God in such a way that our lives can accomplish deeds of spiritual significance? How can we know him so well that we can be assured he will answer our prayer for fire on the altar as he did for the audacious Elijah? How can we come to know God closely enough to interpret the dream of prophecy with confidence like the bold Joseph? How does this intimate knowledge come—the kind that stimulates these exploits?

I am convinced that this kind of knowing comes through a familiarity with the Godhead bred through the hundreds of common incidents in our lives. It is these encounters which God chooses to infuse with his presence *and which we then must take the time to recognize as vehicles of himself*. The bush flamed, if you will remember. It was alive with the Presence, but Moses had to turn aside to see. So must we.

Unfortunately, those of us who call ourselves Christian are all too like the children of Israel, against whom the prophets raved, "You have eyes to see but do not see, and you have ears to hear but you do not hear." Often we hold to the soundest of doctrine but have the emptiest of living. We comprehend the theory, but the translation of the theoretical into the commonplace seems impossible. The truth is known in our heads. But, tragically, it is not incarnate in our being.

After years of wandering in my own wilderness of spirit, I clearly recall when my ears were opened to hear. I had been raised in a lovely Christian home, surrounded by a solid church atmosphere with much emphasis on the written Word—I had memorized seven books of the Bible word-perfect. But one day as I was reading Scripture, I realized I did not understand the meaning of what I was reading. Though I went over the text several times, certain chapters—Hebrews 4 and John 15—were "riddles wrapped in mysteries inside enigmas."

Suddenly, the thought came to me and I had the insight to understand that it was beyond the human: *Karen, you know more than you have experienced*. My ears could hear the voice of One who often speaks in soul-whispers, and I was irrevocably altered. It was true: I knew much, but had touched and lived little. From that moment, my humdrum, ordinary Christianity was set aside in favor of a pursuit of the holy. I became hungry for the reality of God, not merely for precepts about him.

William James, the widely read American philosopher of the nineteenth century, says there are two kinds of knowing: the knowledge about something; and the knowledge of acquaintance. The first knowing is academic understanding, it is classroom dogma, it is theory. The second is experience which touches us where we are living. It is a cologne bottle which we can hold and the affirming words of a parent we can hear and a child's prayer answered word-perfectly, an answer which she can comprehend.

When we talk about wanting a "real relationship with God," what do we mean? I think we are referring to a knowing which falls under the second category. It is certainly what Job meant when he cried, "I *know* whom I have believed!" The measure by which we test deepening spiritual maturity is simple. Is our theory becoming experience? Are we expanding our knowledge of God in the area of acquaintance? Are we, with the organs of the inner man, touching and tasting and hearing and seeing and smelling?

Christ refers to this in a familiar discussion expanded intriguingly by the *Amplified New Testament*. Our Lord says to

Nicodemus, the Jewish leader who came to him secretly by night, "I assure you, most solemnly I tell you, that unless a person is born again (anew, from above), he cannot ever see—know, be acquainted with [and experience]—the kingdom of God."

Being born again is more than just a single event. It is a process, or better yet, it is an event which is the catalyst for a process. It is the procreation of the spirit of the inner man which was once cut off from God, shriveled in death, and is now alive through union with the Holy Spirit. This procreation now enables a once impossible growth process into that spiritual world. We mature spiritually, we know, we can see, we become acquainted with and experience the Kingdom. Spiritual growth is the process of becoming familiar with the supernatural which surrounds us.

As far back into childhood as I can remember, I have always loved Jesus. I can't identify a specific time when I accepted him into my heart, but I have always affirmed him as Savior. At eleven I had, for me, dramatic assurance that I was God's child.

At the age of eighteen I married a minister, and after several years of marriage we moved to Chicago where we soon founded a church on the Near-West side. Located in a teamster's union hall along the rib of a major expressway and beside the underbelly of the sprawling West-Side ghetto, our church ministered to a vast and diverse parish.

Somehow, my childhood faith had no answers for the overwhelming questions posed by the inner city. Missionaries speak of culture shock, that period of adjustment which often occurs when they move from culture to culture. They feel caught for a time between two worlds, and the place they left behind seems more real than their new locale. In the same manner, I went into a profound urban crisis.

It was as though I had left my father's home wearing a party dress totally inappropriate to the new occasion. The suburban Christian culture which had loved me and watched me grow and attended my wedding and sheltered me had not prepared me for the dilemmas of my new dwelling place. My old garment of faith did not fit. Dungarees of some sort, or blue jeans, would have been more suitable. How to make the cloth of Christianity workable? That was the question which haunted me for years.

Where do those hundreds of old men go at night—those who haunt park benches by day and whose major activity seems to be sifting through the trash barrels? How does Christ's love apply to them? What is the immense, unseen condemnation that hovers in the very atmosphere of the inner city, and what is the message of the Kingdom which will lift this pall? Was our neighbor really raped? If she was, what can we do? And if she was not, why does she need to tell this tale, and what can we do? And how do we, who are so few, touch the many hundreds? And what of the filth and the dirt and the waste? And what of the children?

We watched the Near-West side of the city, where our church congregated on Sunday mornings, billow in incendiary flames after the race riots of the sixties, listened in our apartment to the snipers' fire from the nearby housing projects. We closed our windows against tear gas when that generation's anti-establishment young clashed with police in Lincoln Park across from our building, when the forces unleashed during the 1968 Democratic Convention conflagrated on our very block. What was Christ or who were Christ-ones in the face of all this?

Yes, my lovely childhood garment of faith had grown too small—or I had grown too fat. For years I rode on my husband's spiritual coattails. His spirit was flailing and alive, rising each day above the boundaries of naturalism. His faith was real. In the density of urban confusion, David heard the Word.

Finally, there came a time when I began to hunger for a knowing of my own—not a knowledge limited to understanding, but a knowledge in which understanding was fitted to acquaintance. I wanted a knowing of experience. I began searching for a garment of my own, an outfit that would cover my multiple callings—wife, mother, minister, word artisan; something that would be appropriate to wear in the culture in which I now lived.

"You know more than you have experienced," came a whisper to my heart. It was as though God said to me, "It's time you found some coattails of your own!" From that point the theory began to expand into actuality, starting with a period of self-awareness, a coming to terms with myself in a new way, a frank look at the ugly devices of my personality that I had so cunningly hidden. There was finally an abandonment of this being and a plea for incarnation, a cry to be possessed by the knowable Holy Spirit. It was as though the dry and crackling layers of onion skin were slowly peeled away to reveal a juicy and pungent core.

Now it seems as though conversion is always taking place. I am in the eventful process of being born again. It is both a finished and an ongoing work, this coming alive of my spirit. Some seared and barren fields are forever being discovered, then harrowed and furrowed to yield produce. Renaissance is daily occurring within this one soul. I have discovered I am larger within than without—indeed, I am a universe enclosed.

It is clear to me that once I traversed this world which was all aflame with God but I was blinded to the burning bushes. Now, more and more, I am turning aside to see. Perhaps one day I shall be favored like that servant who stood fearfully at Dothan and over whom the prophet Elisha prayed, "O Lord, open his eyes that he may see." His eyes were opened and "behold, the mountain was full of horses and chariots of fire round about . . ."

Yet, to be fair to the work of God within me, I must say that a long journey into spiritual knowing has been made. These workable robes of righteousness are becoming replete with their own splendor. They are becoming familiar, comfortable for chores. Recently, a friend asked, "But do you hear the voice of the Lord speaking to you?" How casually I answered affirmatively, as if there were nothing to it, forgetting for the moment the great discipline and desire, the struggle and duty which have brought me to this place.

"Be careful when you say you 'hear the Lord,' " my husband cautions. I suppose he has visions of Joan of Arc writhing at the stake due to obedience to her "voices." David's counsel comes not out of disbelief but because he knows the difficulty of communicating supernatural things to human understanding. We are sympathetic to the Joans of this world, because a voice often does come, but how to convey through words what occurs is nigh to impossible.

God's voice is not like the announcement imitated by stand-up comics, "Now hear this! Now hear this! This is your Captain speaking!" No, it is a spiritual voice spoken to spiritual ears. This is why it is difficult to explain.

Nor can it be systematized, because it comes in such a variety of ways. It may be our conscience acting as God's messenger. It may be the word of a friend or of an enemy in which God chooses to blaze himself. It may be nature itself shouting forth God. It may be the result of hours and hours spent reading and studying and learning Scripture, with sudden flashing reminders occurring at the most opportune moments. It may be our imaginations leaping with quickened, holy understanding. It may be in the heat of spiritual warfare when we finally choose to stand fast, to fight against what is evil in ourselves or in the world, that we recognize the Presence of heavenly Hosts.

Because it is spiritual, however, this does not mean that it is anything less than real. It is real and it comes in real ways. Our dilemma is to learn to recognize it, to be sensitive to it, then obey it.

My father used to employ the well-worn example of the rose. Daddy would say, "You can take a rose and examine it under a microscope and pull it apart and shred it and pore over it with a magnifying glass. But when you are done, you will no longer have the rose."

Lest I be guilty of examining the rose to pieces, I have chosen to illustrate the whys and the hows of the Word coming unto us rather than to minutely dissect on an academic level the means through which it works. I would rather have the rose and preserve some mystery.

This book is the chronicle of one human's spiritual renaissance, my own. It is about the reflowering, the coming alive, the becoming of one spirit. It is a catalog of my experiences of learning to know God, of growing toward a knowing of *acquaintance*. It is a collection of turning points, a succession of epiphanies.

Actually, these pages have been written in me over the years. My life has served as a tablet on which God has made his markings. These are illustrations of the Word becoming incarnate in a life. Each chapter is a record of his whisper and of my learning to recognize those quiet murmurs. Some were written at the time. Some were written in retrospect. As far as is possible, they are arranged chronologically. All progress toward a heightened understanding of the daily Presence of Christ which, after all, should constitute normal Christianity.

A friend once amazed me by saying, "If you can do it, so can I!" She was referring to my very recent but nevertheless evident spiritual growth. At the time I was surprised that I could be considered any kind of stimulus to her, and more than a little afraid about it. Yet I have come to learn that she was right. We all are windows to one another, through which God's light can shine. My deepest growth has always been excited by saints who demonstrated to me that it is possible to stride the great divide between the natural and the supernatural, between the human and the divine. One human colossus of faith is evidence of what we can all be.

Hopefully, these pages will be a window, one like that pane of glass just recently rubbed by my housewifely efforts. In the sun's glare I can see that it is not quite as polished in the corners as it should be. There is still a child's thumb smudge remaining, and somehow a fresh noseprint from the curious puppy has been planted in its middle. Yet the light's rays still glimmer through it, pouring effusively onto the bedspread, the floor. It is as clear as it needs to be.

I AWAKENING

It is not we who choose to awaken ourselves, but God who chooses to awaken us . . .

— Thomas Merton, *Seeds of Contemplation*

ONE
LAURIE'S MOTHER

She didn't keep her baby. I knew there were women who didn't keep their babies. In fact, this great city hospital with its huge teaching staff had witnessed this drama thousands of times over. But for me, who had been rushed from our suburbs with all the care and concern usually accompanying the birth of a first child, it was a new and terrible awakening.

Here was a woman who would not be keeping her baby—in my hospital room, in the next bed.

The nurse came first, her stern eyes filled with a lack of understanding. "The girl who will be in the next bed is not keeping her baby. Don't-ask-any-questions." She had practically scolded me!

I was stung. It was not my fault she wasn't keeping the baby. Why this ill-directed irritation?

A flurry of nurses shuffled around in the other half of the room, then the curtains were whisked shut. A cart clattered down the hall, stopped. I heard voices—her voice—"Oh, yes, a pack of cigarettes and a TV, please." Someone rummaged with the phone, "Daddy, the baby came. A little girl. I'm fine. Well, you wanted me to call." Her head poked through the drawn drapes. She was in her early thirties. "Hi! You don't have any cigarettes, do you?"

I was politely negative. Not only was she not keeping her baby, but now she would fill the room with smoke and with the junk sounds of television.

She threw back the curtains and pancaked onto her stomach on the bed. I was amazed. It was something I had been longing to do but in my first-time ignorance had been hesitant to try. "Sure," she reported. "With the other ones, the nurses had me on my tummy soon as I delivered. Helps your uterus settle."

Flabbergasted, I viewed her in cold silence. Only the specter of the ugly-eyed nurse's wagging finger kept me from asking if she had kept the other children or had given them away also.

She was kindly in her interest toward me, edgy in the bed. She prattled. Her grammar was imperfect, but her slang was incongruously laced with long words. A television talk show on existentialism piqued her interest, and she filled me in on the meaning of the philosophy to which the program only alluded.

A man, relationship undefined, came to visit several times and she asked him to purchase a box of candy for the nurses. But no family appeared, though she talked of them and held conversations on the phone from time to time.

I heard her reaction to the call from hospital records requesting information for the birth certificate. Having had the same call myself the day before, I eavesdropped and caught her decision to name the baby Laurie. She literally stabbed blind-eyed in that one moment and grabbed this label from the thousands. I knew the next question would be, "Father's name?"

She paused, her assumed jauntiness dropping heavily behind the half-pulled curtain. With what titan did she struggle in that minute of hesitation—anger? revenge? woeful, but wayward, penitence? "None," she answered, then repeated it again to the insistent inquiry on the line's other end, "None."

My heart sank. What kind of babies are named without any agony of forethought? What kind of babies are fathered by none? I thought of David, my firstborn's father, of the rough tweed sport coat, of the foamy lather on the real newday beard, of the dark hair and eyes, of the sturdiness of him, and the annual summer softball charley horse—and of his name, a name to cover, to put in the proper blank on the birth certificate.

Turning in bed, I feigned sleep, but I noticed that she paced the halls that afternoon. How unlikely, this marriage of roommates, this involuntary yoke—she, jittery and jaunty, hiding who-knows-what behind cracked walls of savoir faire; and I, fresh to the world, filled with liberal doses of self-righteousness—protected, untouched.

"You can see the baby once, if you like," said the nurse to Laurie's mother (it was the ugly nurse again). A little swathe enfolding a brown-haired dome was tipped for viewing. The mother who had chosen, for some reason I never questioned, not to keep her infant was tripped, tripped by her instincts. She reached out her hands in yearning, *and I saw it.*

"You want to hold the baby!" said the amazed, the unsympathetic voice. "It's not allowed. You are only allowed to look." The eyes narrowed more sternly.

"No . . . no . . . no . . ." my roommate responded, stumbling emotionally, flailing internally to keep control. "No, I just wanted to see her feet." The tiny toes were unveiled. No questions were asked, and the infant was carried out in the arms of the nurse to—to nevermore.

I saw it. I saw it, Laurie's mother, you who didn't keep your child. I saw you stretch out your arms.

I've thought of you a million times, you whom I so glibly labeled as common. I've seen you in a thousand photographs, your arms outstretched. Arms outstretched—mothers grieving for mangled bodies, sons in plastic beneath coffins draped with nations' flags. Arms outstretched, for little faces pressed against glass, human giveaways before the rushing onslaught of inhuman holocausts. Arms outstretched —infants abandoned on doorsteps, scraps of paper pinned over their hearts reading, "Please take care of my baby."

You held out your arms. No matter the circumstances. No matter the answers to questions unasked. No matter the nevermores. This was your child, your infant of pain, your Laurie. You wanted to hold, to love. You wanted it at once.

If I could have loved you then as I love you now, if I could have spoken the word which would have assuaged your desperation, would those outstretched arms have found something to hold? You were not common; a flame flickered in you unexpectedly. If only *my* eyes had bespoken gentle, tender caring. If only I had not been smug, could I have satisfied your outstretched longing?

Thank you, Laurie's mother, for sharing my room. Thank you for the rare insight you gave me about women who don't keep their babies. Thank you for beginning the lesson in me which God is now completing, the truth that he has created no ordinary people—it is only we humans who make them (or ourselves) so.

I, too, lift hands these days,
for all those women with
arms outstretched.
Amen.

TWO
NOTHING AT ALL

I suppose the entourage to the hospital when our firstborn arrived *was* a bit excessive. Both grandparents-to-be got into the act for the hour's drive from our western suburb to the medical center in the city resting on the edge of the lake. David sat at my side in the back seat (it being judged he would be too nervous to drive safely). One set of parents were in the front of our vehicle while the others followed in hot pursuit in another car (in case ours broke down).

All three of our boys have delayed their nativities by exactly two weeks, growing larger and rounder and fully ripe within. It was only our daughter who had the decency to arrive early and the consideration not to be born on the first day of the week. Our sons have all arrived at the most inappropriate time for a minister—on Sundays. I have replied more than once to the typical, "Your husband may come in now," with, "Oh, no! Don't bother him! He's still working on his sermon!"

With the last child, I remember being perched on the delivery table, looking at the wall clock which showed 9:00 A.M. and asking, "Do you think we can get this baby born in time for his father to see him and make it to church?"

"When does your service start?" replied my considerate obstetrician, pulling on his surgical gloves.

"In a half hour," said I.

"I don't see why not," said he.

So the baby was born at 9:10 and dutifully viewed by his father, who then raced across town to step behind the pulpit at exactly 9:30.

Our first child, a boy, most unusually waited to arrive until after the morning service. On the way to the hospital, whichever parent was driving in our little motorcade turned and asked, "Shall we take the shortcut or drive down Michigan Ave.?"

"Oh, Michigan Avenue," I answered. If I'm dying and being rushed somewhere in an ambulance, I hope someone will care enough to let me direct him down that broad boulevard I love in all kinds of Chicago weather, day or night, any season. So past the Art Institute we drove, past the tall obelisks of buildings, past the Water Tower which survived the Great Fire, onto Lake Shore Drive bordered with water and sand and parks, to the emergency entrance of the hospital.

The only objects worth noticing in the small labor cell were the clock on the wall, whose hands didn't seem to move at all, and a nurse standing close to my prone head. So tall and white, she seemed to be the symbol of something unrevealed. Only her thick Irish brogue protested humanity.

Despite wives' tales and nervous parents, my labor was invaded by a holy calm. No husband or doctor or drug could have afforded me such an unworldly interlude. Looking back, I can recognize that it was the Presence of the Lord, because all the crises of my life have since been dominated by this quiet, peaceful certainty. At the time I thought it was due to the angel in white who stood above my head and rolled her Irish "r's" in soothing words of comfort.

A scream ripped the corridor, ricochetted off the wall, and moved into the serenity of my own pain, where it was absorbed. "Poor thing," whispered the soft voice. "Saw them bring her in, I did. Elderly man an' his woman. Little bit o' a thing. Can't be over fifteen." The scream again. "Scared t'death. They left her."

"Can't you help her?" I whispered beneath my own hurt. "Sure 'n not," she smiled. "I'm here t' help you."

So I began to pray, all twenty years of me praying for the fifteen-year-old screaming in terror outside my door.

Someone had waited too long. She delivered her baby in that hall, poor child, with feet sounding on tile, metallic wheels hurrying, and no one to hold her hand.

"Such a big baby," people said to me later. "Didn't you have a hard time?"

"No," I always replied. "It was nothing."

Not until I was being examined before the birth of my fourth child did I hear my doctor mumbling as he was making notations in my growing folder of records, "You had quite a rough time with that first baby."

"Oh, really?" I responded, a little surprised.

He continued to murmur in his most doctorly fashion about "large size, over ten pounds, first delivery, turned position, elevated blood pressure..."

Suddenly, I remembered my husband reporting the comment of the resident doctor (who hadn't enough experience to realize he should reassure an untried father about the condition of his wife and the perfection of his newborn): "It was really rough. I don't think he'll let her go through one like that again."

Yet, all I remember was the Presence and that still, still room. It truly seemed like nothing at all.

I lost my way in this city,
I lost my way.
It was not the frantic panic
of a child who
finds that his mother's hand has
disappeared,
and his head is scarcely taller
than store counters—but
more the dead-end ennui
of a rat in a maze
meeting nothing but no-exits,
walls, and detours.
I lost my way in this city,
I lost my way.
Not in pointless meanderings
on avenues,
along nameless streets and alleys,
but in spirit.
I wandered, searching for vital signs
in my faint soul,
wondering what condemnation
had been posted.

THREE
THE CENTER

Like my small sons who endlessly drag home straggly sticks
and branches, nondescript stones and chunks of concrete,
I have a passion for the simple, the commonplace. The
everyday has special meaning in our eyes. It is precious to us
and we are the inveterate collectors of all those things
which any man may have for the asking—of those things
which belong to no one in particular and therefore to anyone
who will possess them.

This all began when we moved from the suburbs to go
minister in the city—that wonder which I love and hate. *This
is the center of the world*, I thought. *All paths converge here.*

After a while it pressed too close, too many people breathed
the same air, too much movement filled the same spaces.
No quiet. No resting. "Why don't you get away for the day,"
my husband would suggest, sensing my edginess.

Quite right. All I need is to see a horizon. In the city,
buildings obscure the boundary between earth and sky.
Twenty miles from here, I can watch the sun set, see the stars
in the great black height. Stars rarely show through the
city's artificial illumination; we see only the blinking of
airplanes circling in pattern before landing at O'Hare, or the
fluorescent glare of the ring at the top of the Hancock building.

So I would go for a day and return bringing a part of the
country home to the city—citrine hedge apples from trees

which thornily fence some old pasture, or stalks of wheat to
bind with velour ribbon for the front door, or teasel and
hydrangea—perfect for dried bouquets. Somehow, collecting
these treasures always brought restfulness to my soul.

My latest discovery was a desolate strand of swamp grass.
"Stop! Stop the car!" I cried to a bewildered sister-in-law.
Dodging the trucks and whizzing vehicles, I dashed across the
highway, enduring the curious glare of construction
workers, and began to pull at the tough stems. Frantically,
I collected all I dared, nervous that someone might stop
me in my hoarding.

Later, while arranging the delicate fronds on their slender
reeds in an old crock, I wondered about the source of
this almost physical need to fill our apartment with the natural
world I encounter.

Many women would ridicule my baskets of weeds which
shed seeds on freshly vacuumed carpets. They would disdain
my treasures which collect dust and provide clutter. I only
know I must bring home a part of where I have been. It is
a variation of the philosopher's theme: I think, therefore I am.
Rather, my collecting seems to declare: It is here, therefore
it happened.

I have an irresistible urge to trap, like a time-lapse photo,
the inevitable progression of life—a milkweed pod bursting
into a clump of baby-fine hair, a lilac branch, hard nub
buds near opening. The mental images which I recall in order
to restore calm from chaos are of the unseen wind shafting
a field of tall grasses, all moving in suddenness to instant
choreography; of early winter's dull, muted melancholy;
of the migration of the monarch butterflies, resting for one
cosmic moment on a weathered cottonwood tree. Yet, I must
have more than just memories, I must have something
physical, something to hold, to handle.

By collecting my own samples of the everyday, I pay
nothing. To have to pay for a part of the world which belongs
to all would be an affront to my senses. I refuse to buy
the springtime pussy willows in some downtown florist shop.
I must discover them myself, then plunge over fences
and through muck and cut my fingers in the taking—and see
the thwarted sky—blue it would be, but it's gray today—

and feel the damp whisper of summer warmth to come,
and view the wild irregularities of the weed, the stems
crisscrossing in diagonals of abstract design. To pay would
deny me the experience!

I never pass my oval basket loaded with large shells without
being momentarily transported... Once, after working
a grueling three weeks in Venezuela, my husband and I were
scheduled for a few days' layover on the tiny Netherland
Antilles island of Aruba. We baked out our weariness on
bleached beaches, floated in the amazingly clear Caribbean
(while bumper stickers at home pleaded, "HELP SAVE
OUR LAKE"), our minds suspended in thoughtlessness like
the bobbing sea urchins we saw below.

These shells which now hear the cry of another sea—of
sirens, traffic, and humanity—we unearthed ourselves and
washed endlessly. Each time I pass them I regain a momentary
impression—of sea salt, or the flap of a pelican's flight,
or a trade wind which blew us beyond ourselves.

Another working trip, to Florida this time, yielded four
mesh bags of grapefruit and oranges which I picked
myself in my host's grove—and where I heard the mocking-
bird's cry, where the bougainvillea and azalea were in lush,
fragrant bloom, where the bright warmth pushed away
the remembered shadows of a midwestern February. "How
will you get everything on the plane?" my hostess laughed,
eyeing the additional grocery sack filled with huge pine
cones. "She'll get them home," said my patient, long-
enduring husband. "My wife has a thing about bringing the
world back."

Having lived in the city for two years, we found our busy
lives left us little time for assessment. *We were certainly
at the center of the world*. Our Old Town apartment was planted
in the rich soil of an incredible community. Here seemingly
disparate patches were cross-stitched to each other in a
crazy quilt of illogical design. The drug culture descended and
designated our little triangle of a neighborhood as its
capital. We became an artist's colony where well-clad
suburban matrons mingled with the bearded and the barefoot,
all shopping (or mooching) in the boutiques and food stores
and galleries. Affluent city professionals bought historic

old graystones to restore just blocks from acres and acres of settlement housing.

Many young couples from our slice of city sent their children, garbed in blue blazers, to private or parochial schools, while others grabbed what learning they could under the auspices of the Public Board of Education. Amazingly to me, in uniform or out of it, all the children developed an uncanny street savvy. They all had the ability to arrive at the destination toward which they had started! They boarded the right buses and elevated trains. Nonchalantly, they hailed taxis. They made proper transfers, without hesitancy, understood why the buildings were numbered the way they were, and instinctively sensed which neighborhoods to avoid. My greatest fear was of being carried by the Chicago Transit Authority to some terminal from which there was no return.

The bums of Clark Street crept to the perimeter of our locale; the chicken man rode the bus with us, his rooster tucked snugly under his elbow. We watched the self-appointed pigeon keeper making daily trips, pumping his three-wheel bicycle, its back basket stuffed with peanuts in a burlap sack, his sole enterprise the nourishment of the city's already overstuffed feathered denizens. The parapets of the Gold Coast lifted our heads, their dwellers urban magicians understanding the secret wizardry of wealth and power. Long, lean athletes loped easily beside mammoth dogs in the park. Gentle philosophers played chess in open-air lakeside pavilions. On what a variable, yet savory, visual goulash we feasted!

Meals, in particular, stand out in my mind—not so much what we ate, but with whom. A bishop of the Catholic Church in Vietnam came to dinner and mourned the doctrines of U.S. administration officials which he felt had paved the way for the conflagration in his country. We had afternoon tea with members of the Chicago Historical Society and supped with new acquaintances in their eighty-fifth-floor apartment in a landmark edifice, where we discussed the paradoxical nature of truth.

We were the guests at the Thanksgiving feast of a family living in one of the vast low-income housing projects. Our

host met us on the ground floor, warned us to watch
for falling missiles thrown from upper-story balconies,
accompanied us up the elevator (and down when we were
ready to leave), then warmly pulled aside the steel grate that
protected his front door and welcomed us into his concrete-
block walled rooms. There his children called me Teacher—
"Teacha, Teacha, come see this. This is my bed, our room."
And there his wife said softly, her Southern accent gently
slurred, "You make me proud to have you come to my home."
Bright badges, they all are, pinned now to my memory.

*We are at the center of the world, at the hub of its most frenetic
and intriguing activity.*

After we had immersed ourselves in the city for several
years, laboring in much agony and ecstasy to give birth to a
newborn church, one day we escaped to the country to
treat my husband's mother to a special dinner. It was Mother's
Day, and dining at a little restaurant hidden away in a
rural area, I had to blink my eyes against the brilliance of the
green and contain my heart against the soft sweet pull of
May. I returned to the city, stunned. I had forgotten the spring.

In the city, where only summer and winter occur, it is easy
to forget the spring and fall. If one forgets the spring,
it is easy to forget what is not made by human hands, what is
not formed from steel or girders or concrete. It is easy
to forget what is natural, what is beyond the human.

Suddenly, I understood my inveterate collecting. It was an
unconscious expression of my deep need for reminders
of the supernatural. I had lost my way in this city. I had come
adrift from my spiritual moorings. I had made a substitution
—the wonder of the city for the wonder of nature.

These common things—the pressed Queen Anne's lace, the
dark dandelion leaves, this beach stone, these rushes—these
were my mementos, barriers held against a city which
was consuming me. It was not the center of the world. These
simple things—the violet blooming forever under glass,
the fossil bookending children's volumes—were enjoinders
against my absorption with urbanity. They all bespoke:
there is something deeper, something more, something
farther on, something better.

There are country fields unmarked by concrete walkways

where spongy mud captures exploring shoes, and thistles catch on clothing. There is thorny wild blackberry picking. There are ponds where children can drown if they're not careful. There are pheasant hens flushed from hollow grassy broods. These are not the center either, but somehow the natural things seem closer to it.

This is the ultimate danger inherent in our humanity, always to assume that whatever it is we do, whatever it is that absorbs us, wherever we live and with whomever we live, that these things are the center of the world. Our professions, whether business or science or homemaking, become primary. Our relationships, whether with children or spouses or colleagues, become preeminent. Hidden from us is the fact that another world exists, where the center truly is.

In each of us is a germ that can hatch into a disease of substitutions. Anything that preoccupies our attention can eventually slip into that cavity in our souls and attempt to fill the spot that was meant only for One Other to indwell.

As much as I love the city which moves me and woos me and frightens me, it is not all. My baskets and shelves and vases are filled with mute testimonies to the truth which was stamped in childhood on my subconscious. They are winsome, gentle, instinctive warnings that there is something beyond the human. This inveterate collecting is an unconscious expression of need, a need for spring—indeed, a need for a wellspring.

There is another center. The center is never here for any of us, not in these rooms, not in these lives, not in the dominating fascination of this world. The center is always beyond where we are, and many of us must journey on anguished odysseys before we reach it.

FOUR
PRAYERS FOR THE BODY—1970

IN THE TEAMSTER'S UNION HALL
WHICH SERVES AS OUR CHURCH SANCTUARY

Help us not to care, Lord, that there is no altar here, no cantilevered ceiling, no magenta carpeting. Let your Spirit impress us more than the distracting footsteps of latecomers on the bare ballroom floor, more than the cry of babies from the nearby ladies' lounge.
May the differences of our skins and cultures and the variations of our intellectual viewpoints not be dividing factors. May they unite us.

TWO YOUNG FACES—ONE DEFINED BY GRANNY GLASSES

Father, you have recently met them in conversion. (No doubt they know far too much of this world's experiences. But the box they brought to church contained five dozen homemade doughnuts for our fellowship hour. One girl has led her sister to the Lord already! Their conversation is dated either "before we found God" or "after we found God." After accepting Christ, one of the girls gave away a carefully hoarded package of marijuana to an amazed friend. She said she didn't need it anymore.)

A BLACK WHO INTRODUCES HIMSELF AS A REVOLUTIONARY

(I wanted to say, "We hope you'll feel at home here, because we feel 'revolutionary' ourselves, like a certain brand of ecclesiastical revolutionaries." How could he understand?

How could he know how dramatically all our lives are being changed, revolutionized, by the power of Christ's Spirit within, and that it is this force which is moving us to attempt to touch a city with methods and means that may seem strange to our church fathers? Sometimes it is hard to know what to say to people. Perhaps he's from the radical Black Panther office, just a few blocks away.)

THE COFFEE HOUSE WORKERS
WHO CLOSED THEIR DOORS AT FIVE THIS MORNING

(The girls are still in jeans. We're so thankful they make the effort to get to church after the strenuous evening and the morning cleanup, that it doesn't matter what they wear. Besides, half the regular membership of this church wears jeans on Sunday morning!)

Father, give wisdom as your Word is preached. Give special meaning to these kids as they try to relate Christianity to twentieth-century ideologies and philosophies. (Those kids are barefoot.) *All these hippie types, some from conservative, traditional churchgoing homes. Help those with shattered personalities and those with discontinued lives and those being whirled to pieces in a maelstrom of rebellion.*

THE MIDDLE-AGED COUPLE
WHOSE DAUGHTER HAS BLOWN HER MIND ON DRUGS

God, wherever that young girl is, draw her unto you. Speak to the father, bewildered and broken, as you have spoken to his wife. By your grace, give them both the peace they are seeking.

THE MEDICAL CENTER PERSONNEL

(The interns and residents and technicians—) *Help us to stabilize their science-oriented training, training which demands proof in order to accept your existence. Faith is often the antithesis of proof.* (I wish we could find him a wife! He wrote the loveliest thank-you note after dinner in our home.) *Thank you for using his simple act to sustain me.*

(The nurses—there have been so many. One, now married, just had twins. She met her husband around our dining table. Another writes from the war zone in Vietnam. Still another called long distance in the middle of the night asking for prayer.)

THE CHILD OF THE GHETTO, SITTING BESIDE ME

(He's strong and husky. Something is dripping from his gym shoes! "What is that?" I whisper. His answer verifies my suspicions, "Tar." We are tutoring close to a hundred of these children. Our young people go into the homes, creating an unfamiliar blend of contrasting lives.

("This is Mark," our neighborhood contact explains. "He's EMH." But I doubt that, Mark. Your bright eyes deny that classification. If anything, you're gifted—and unmanageable. Educable Mentally Handicapped—too often the label is an inner-city "solution" to behavior problems.)

God, we know that children are of inestimable value to your Son. He broke his exacting schedules and the adult agendas of his companions to bless them. He instructed us to be like little children. What is to become of these thousands, beautiful beyond words? Lord, are you taking responsibility for them?

THOSE WHO ARE NOT HERE

Lord, city work is always a matter of taking two steps forward for every three backwards. Where are those who have turned away, the ones we've lost? (Where is the psychology major who first considered Christ, then rejected him? Where is the neighborhood family that has stopped attending? And the student couple from the University of Illinois Circle Campus— she professed faith in Christ, but he did not. Where are they all?)

THE WEARER OF A
BRILLIANT PURPLE SARI IN THE CONGREGATION

(How lovely. It is an unconscious adornment to our worship. In fact, this whole congregation is a colorful lot!) *But what a delightful gift this blaze of purple is from your hand, a celebrative banner this Sunday morning.* (What is the story of that Indian couple? They are among the thousands who study in our urban university centers and attend the church because of our outreach with internationals.)

THE JANITOR WHO OFTEN ASSISTS IN USHERING

(He is employed by the Teamsters' Union, who allow us to meet in their building. He is here Sunday after Sunday.) *Keep his heart open to the message of your love.*

THE COMMUNITY OF OUR WORSHIP
(How bound we are to one another, and yet how diverse.)
O Lord, can you keep us together? Can we experience adoration as a corporate unit? Can you give us the beauty of community, of common lives, of shared living in the face of all that can pull us apart?

There is one body, and one spirit... one Lord, one faith, one baptism, one God and Father of all, who is above all, and through all, and in you all.

Ephesians 4:4, 5, 6

THE INNER CITY
Interject your voice, Father, above the noise of the elevated train that rattles outside our windows, above the police and ambulance sirens that whine toward the hospitals across the expressway. Insert your Presence above the human anguish, the quiet desperation. The city itself is our competition—it is also our parish!

FIVE
THE SIGHS OF THE CITY

Every time I close my eyes, I hear the city's sighs. I suppose she will be with me the rest of my life, no matter where I live, however much I attempt to obliterate her cries. No matter in which hills I hide, she will creep up on me when I am in repose, breaking my cherished solitude, and she will heave upon me her mighty breath.

Images of her are pricked like braille to the underside of my tight-lidded eyes, and often before falling asleep, she is the last thing I see. A negative photographic plate of her is imprinted on me, her black buildings outlined in flashes of lurid, neon light.

She will always tear me with what I know of her—in her, beauty and horror cohabit and bring forth their progeny, bestiality and lonely good.

Eyes shut, I can hear her roaring behind my stillness. She is never silent, but ever going. Her sirens constantly staccato the quiet, making me shudder to imagine the terror each one represents. Her wheels are eternally turning. The patterned rhythms of sound—laughter, shrieking, shouting intermingle with the language of metal—crunching, squalling, cranking, pounding—and they all pay noisy homage to their dark Landlord who is never an absentee.

Somewhere sobbing fills a room, then blows mournful breath into the wind which falls out from mushroomed sorrow

over every district. The night waits, a moan-filled quarry
to store all the motion, noise, and anguish the city-day
cannot contain.

She roars to drown the silence, then sighs. And every time
I close my eyes, I can hear her sigh. It is a sound of longing—
for the yeast, the salt, the light. I have ears to hear the
tuned steel teeth of the music bar which revolves in the boxed
underparts of my lids, my heart, my mind. Never to be
forgotten is the mechanical revolving cylinder sounding the
city's sobbed sighs.

SIX
THE ENEMY DESPAIR

Having heard David's sermon on temptation repeated
numerous times, I could almost deliver it from heart myself.
The text was from *The Living Bible*, 1 Peter 5:8:

*Be careful—watch out for attacks from Satan, your great enemy.
He prowls around like a hungry, roaring lion, looking for some
victim to tear apart. Stand firm when he attacks. Trust the Lord.*

The sermon's three points were simple enough: "1. Satan's
desire is to destroy you. 2. Your opportunity is to overcome.
3. God's promise is his presence." I had even edited the
manuscript into article form.

It wasn't until one long February (it is not the shortest
month of the year for some of us) when the winter slush, the
interminably gray Great Lake skies overcast my own spirit for
twenty-eight days, that I realized I was in some icy
solstice of the soul, looking my adversary in the face. With
a start, I realized—he did want to destroy me, and through
my destruction wreak havoc in the lives of the children,
and ultimately damage my husband's vital ministry. *His desire
was to destroy me*.

I can't remember exactly when the depressions began, and
by "depression" I mean a debilitating gloom of the psyche
which renders one nonfunctional. I am not referring to

vague feelings of discontent, or to having a lousy mood. I
mean waking in the morning and barely being able to lift one's
head from a pillow, feeling the heavy hood of some medieval
falconer blinding my soul's eyes, his rope tethering my
emotions. I mean facing the day with dread because the minor
functions seem to be impossible. Making beds and doing
dishes and combing one's hair are vehicles for a confusing
desperation. The made bed looks lumpy and welted,
corrugated with wrinkles. The washed dish is spotted and
sooted, the dishwater slime. Combed hair is a web of
cobstrands, dusty and lusterless. The mirror reveals splotches
and ugliness.

Why try? Don't do it again. Everything you turn your hand
to is failure. You are failure. Your very breath is stale, stale life.

There truly was a pit of darkness into which I was
descending.

It seems amazing now to realize that my own husband and
family were unaware of my descent. Yet unless one has
experienced desperation, it is easy to overlook the symptoms
in others.

When the mood had done its work, I was released,
springing vitally into life, into the sweetness of each breath-
beat, into the glow of the children's eyes and the beauty
of my husband, into the world of people and activities. The
darkness was forgotten and I learned to keep the despair
to myself, because I didn't know how to speak of it, nor did I
realize where it was tunneling.

Perhaps the moods began in high school. I can remember
beginning the days consciously attempting to be the model of
a joyous Christian teen. Smiles wreathed my face, cheery
hellos were given to all who passed in the halls, I acted
out perky and positive attitudes. By midmorning, however,
the droop was on the bloom from all this effort. I usually
dragged home and flopped into bed until dinner.

Early in our marriage a pattern seemed to emerge. Married
at eighteen to a man seven years older, I stepped from
the shelter of my family to the shelter of my husband. There
was little time for balanced personality development;
my adult maturity had to occur within the confines of our
marriage, and within a few years my growing room was

crowded by cumulative pregnancies and the responsibilities of child rearing. I began to experience crying jags, inarticulate effusions of frustration that left my husband helpless and myself drained.

"I can't do anything well!" I would weep. It was true; a little bit of this and a little bit of that, detours into crafts, but no discipline into art. Stepping from the refuge of my father's home to the refuge of my husband's, there had been no time to develop specialties, and I lacked the personal fortitude to become anything's master. This was an area of vulnerability of which the crafty prey-monger took note.

I also felt as though I had no friends, no one apart from family who really liked me. Girl friends from high school were still in college, and obviously, the boyfriends were no longer calling. Our acquaintances were mostly David's colleagues, and their wives were the *mothers* of many of my former friends. I often felt caught between our ages, hurrying to catch up to David's maturity, leaving behind something undone, having a baby here and a baby there, not sure of how old I really was, and certainly unable to peg a peer group. Here was the other potential trouble spot. If I had no friends, wasn't it because I was unlovable? Wasn't it because there was something basically repugnant about me?

Through the years I began to experience periodic, though unpredictable, visitations. Something was gnarling my twenty-some-year-old being into ugliness. Admittedly, there was a part of me that loved these orgies of self-pity, so in a way I opened the door of my spirit to a malignant artist painting his meaningless impressions in my inner chambers. Seemingly without cause he would come, this lover of despair, stretching his stays from afternoons to days, until he embraced my soul for weeks before going. Finally on a desperate February day he wearied me fully and somehow David's words, which I had heard so often, broke through the clouded gloom.

There had been wispy thoughts of suicide that month—*wouldn't I be doing everyone a favor if life just ended*—which as yet hadn't had a chance to possess me. *Which would be the easiest and most painless way?* These lingering vapors were only introductions to a hell through which I did not have to walk;

but they fogged my mind as the blackness increased, until on some days it seemed an effort to breathe, despair had so polluted my inner air.

I hated myself for my ennui, for the dirty house, for the fact that no friends called or cared. Ugly, ugly, ugly be his name. Praise to me in my all-consuming ugliness. Think of Karen; dislike Karen. Adore this awfulness. Don't lift your head; stay in bed today. If you struggle in this grasp you will only go deeper into the muck, the black February muck of winter.

It came with clarity and life, the thought—*he wants to destroy me. David was right, Satan's desire is to destroy us.*

Suddenly I could see the implications of my despair. The children's lives could be ruined, their mother unresponsive to their needs and eventually resenting and hating their natural demands. Perhaps suicide, or huge psychological treatment expenses which would keep David from functioning in his ministry. It would ruin my parents if I died in this despair. The waves rippled on and on. *Satan's desire was to destroy me.*

Something called to me at that moment of realization. I think its name was Love. It asked me to choose. Which did I care for most? Children, husband, family, or the desperate wraith of my soul? The answer was obvious. But did I love them enough to struggle to preserve myself and them also? For the first time in my life, I consciously committed myself to spiritual warfare. I was determined that if there was power in Christ, I would find a way to escape the hold of the destroyer.

Recalling part two of David's sermon, I realized it was my opportunity to overcome. My Christian background hadn't counted as nothing in my life. As a child I had memorized 1 Corinthians 10:13:

No temptation has overtaken you that is not common to man. God is faithful, and he will not let you be tempted beyond your strength, but with the temptation will also provide the way of escape, that you may be able to endure it.

I knew the words of truth; my problem was how to experience them.

I decided I would catch the enemy when he turned the handle on the door to my soul, rather than after he had dirtied the rooms with a few days' sojourn. The worst thing about depression is it sets off dominoes of emotional traumas. It is like the back injury that causes pain to be felt in the neck, although the ailment itself is located somewhere along the lower vertebrae. Helpless to discover the source of depression now that despair's boa-embrace had severed my nerve endings, I resolved to stop everything the moment I heard the doorknobs jiggling.

When I sensed myself sinking lower than my normal moods, I would sit still and ask, "Now what is it that is causing me to feel this way? What has someone said that has discouraged me? or what have I said that I'm embarrassed about? Do I feel that David is too busy to give me attention? Am I really resentful? or am I physically exhausted and making more of things than they call for?"

I discovered that there was always a hook on which my adversary could hang his cloak.

Once the source of my growing uneasiness was discovered, it became a matter of refusing the enemy an entry. It became an intense battle to "stand firm." It felt literally as though I were pressing my weight against a door while something heaved and shoved on the other side. I can remember fighting against giving way to my unhealthy feelings, sometimes for hours. "I refuse the power of the enemy," I would whisper, teeth clenched. "I refuse to give in to this thing which he wants to use to destroy me."

I would force myself to keep on functioning. Keep cleaning, keep working. Get out of the house, go to the beach, to the zoo. If you are tired, go to bed and sleep. Don't allow yourself to brood; above all else, keep that door shut.

One morning, after several months of this off-and-on struggle, I had been in conflict for hours. Standing before the kitchen sink, tears streamed down my cheeks and dropped into the dishwater. I was weary with the heat of warfare, and certain I would go under without reinforcements.

"O God," I prayed, "I'm trying to refuse the power of the enemy in my life. I know he wants to destroy me. I have fought him over the last few months and all this morning. You have said you won't let us go through anything you don't think we are able to endure. I don't think I can endure any more of this. David says your promise is your Presence. I can't keep my back against this door anymore. If you don't help me, I'm gone." For a half hour I repeated: Help me, please help me. Oh, help, God. Please help.

Soon I noticed that the door was at rest, the knob no longer turned, and when I peeked out, the black cloak had disappeared from the hook in the outer hallway.

By some insight of the Holy Spirit, some rare precognition, I knew that despair was gone for good. Though I had experienced depression in its minor and more severe forms for some eight years, *I have never tasted it again since that day.* It was the first evidence in my life of the practical, redemptive power of God, of his ability to deliver us from the teeth of temptation.

I was not so naive as to think my responsibility for personal mental health was over. There were long-range life changes I had to effect. The process of building a whole person was about to begin; the armor of my self-image had huge holes which left me vulnerable to the enemy's fiery darts. There was mending to do, rebuilding of the chain mail, a new insignia to be painted on my shield, a sword to be forged. Yet I knew the depression was gone, defeated by my Overlord. Instinctively, I was aware a battle lull had been provided for me to spend in preparation, garrisoning, and foraging for provender.

Many have been the lessons in knowing I've learned since that day; many have been the failures and successes. When I grow weary, my knees aching, my arms weary, when my vision seems blurred—I think back to the sink and my tears splashing in the water, back to my plea for God's Presence, back to the instant knowledge that he had truly and finally vanquished my despair.

This buoys me, sustains me, lifts me up. It is my personal miracle of the Red Sea crossing, my water gushing from the rock, my pillar of fire by night. God's promise *is* his Presence.

SEVEN
BE ANGRY AND SIN NOT

One morning I woke enraged with God!

The night before, my husband had come home from a
church council meeting with the usual tale of woe. Every
congregation has a resident grouch—each name and face is
different, but this person is always opposed, on principle, to
anything. Ours was practicing his negative minority
leadership. (I once sighed to my mother-in-law, "If lay people
only knew what damage they do to men in ministry." Her
reply as she sighed back to me was a wise reminder, "If men in
ministry only knew what damage they do to the lay people"!)

At any rate, this night David and I joined in prayer for our
friend, requesting a special kind of love. We experienced
a resolve that enabled us to sleep soundly, but I woke the next
morning, a bleak winter day, in a barely suppressed rage!

Fuming down the stairs, I banged cupboards, stomped
around, clattering utensils, and spoke tight-lipped to the
children. This may sound childish to some and perhaps it is,
but for me it was much preferable to the inward silent
corrosiveness of unexpressed depression. Angry Februaries
are much healthier than suicidal ones!

I was learning that anger could be positive if it was not
ill-used. It is external, directing energy out of oneself.
It vents the brackish bitters that have a tendency to clog the
inward valves and systems, bringing release. Used wisely,

it can be motivational. It is righteous anger that cleanses
temples and defies injustices, that expresses a muddled
thought with sudden lucidity, exuberance. The difficulty, of
course, is to learn to use it well.

On this morning, however, my husband was unaware of all
these obvious benefits of living with an angry woman.
Cautiously, he peered around the kitchen doorpost and
tested, "Something wrong with you today?" Pin a medal on
that brave man. He must have known that all the winged
frenzies would erupt if he lifted the lid off this box.

Human behaviorists tell us that one of the most successful
ways to overcome a negative habit is to substitute a positive
one in its place. For me anger was more positive than
depression, and at this time in my life it had become a
necessary emotional substitute. In fact, when I began to
examine my depressions closely, I discovered many a
simmering pot of peeve. I have since learned that some
psychologists regard depression as just a case of suppressed
anger. Something about that routine church meeting had
lifted the lid from some internal boiling kettle of chowder, and
rather than clamping it back on, I was allowing the soup
to boil over.

My husband received more than he deserved. I went on and
on—I was tired of the church, tired of the scrimping, tired of
the people. I was tired of the yearly finance committee
that evaluated our salary and made us somehow feel guilty for
putting in only a sixty-hour work week! I'd had enough of
the whole thing!

Coming to terms with anger is always painful for the
persons with whom we live. We may subject them to frequent
theatrical displays, unexpected fireworks, and just some
plain, general unpleasantness. Yet those unpleasant initial
explosions that occur in the process of self-knowledge are
often good, because they are like cleansing forays of the
psyche. We discover pantries fully stocked with venom, and
begin to get rid of all this garbage. Unfortunately, we often
dump it on the innocent bystander nearby, and for many
of us that means a family member. This is called displaced
anger, and this dislocation of our fury is generally part
of the process of learning to use anger well.

As difficult as all this may seem, again I must emphasize that it is much healthier than the mute moping of depression, the anguished spiraling inward, the wispy thoughts of death and dying. I view it as the early steps to health. Many an angry woman dwells within the family of the church, and often one of them is the pastor's wife.

"And furthermore," I continued on that angry day, as bleak as the weather outside. "Furthermore, we have never had a real vacation. I'm tired of going places where you work your head off speaking, and I stay in a cabin with ten junior highers! We're both weary beyond words and we need a rest. I *obviously* need a rest. Now what are you going to do about it?"

I could tell that David was imperceptibly inching back down the hall. "Now whose fault is that?" he reasoned. When will the logicians of this world learn they cannot apply logic to runaway emotion! "You know we don't have any money." It was true. Our last twenty dollars (along with pennies and dimes and nickels from the children's piggy banks) had been contributed toward paying a friend's bail bond, but that fact did not turn my anger.

"It's God's fault!" I pronounced. "He knows we're worn out, that we've never had a *real* vacation, that we have *given* our money away, that we are trying to put his Kingdom *first*. It's God's fault. Now either he's who he says he is—or he's not! Either he takes care of those who serve him or he doesn't!"

There, it was out. This was the true cause of all that bewildering emotion. It wasn't the church or the council or the finance committee or the resident grouch. They had become targets for my displaced anger. I had finally sipped the stew and identified its real ingredients. Deep down, I was bitterly resentful toward God. He wasn't taking care of us the way I thought he should. In fact, I was enraged with him.

David turned slightly white, laid down his shield of reason, and resorted to retreat, leaving me in the kitchen sullenly ticking off the names of all the people I knew who were going to Europe or the Bahamas or Florida. They were all businessmen or doctors, as far as I could tell. Not a minister in the lot. Humph, fine God we'd hooked ourselves up with. Fine promise—"Put ye first the kingdom of God and his righteousness and *all* these things shall be added unto you..."!

My outburst tapped some of the strength from my rage and we continued with the day's routine—David with administrative paperwork and I with the endless repetition of a mother's chores. After a little while the front doorbell rang and a huge box was delivered containing bright, lush oranges and grapefruit with a note written in the welcome handwriting of a close friend: "A little bit of Florida sunshine for you—"

"Well, it's not a vacation..." David began, then stopped. I could see he was trying to stifle the laughter swelling inside of him, thinking that if reason hadn't worked, humor would certainly stoke my flames even higher. He didn't need to say a thing. I *knew* what he was thinking. Our vacations had been gifts from God, ways to travel on limited funds. Our small children had immensely enjoyed all the summer camps where he had been invited to speak. They had taken advantage of the horseback riding, swimming holes, and archery lessons. I had only bunked with junior highers once, and after I got over my initial huff, I had come to love them.

"Well, it's not a vacation..." David started again. Then he laughed—out loud.

Usually, I am mollified by laughter, but not this time. It was not my husband's lack of sensitivity in howling before my distress that goaded me, however, it was the distinct impression I had that God was laughing at me too, that he was sniggering at me behind his hand.

Drawing my dignity around me as best I could, I looked David straight in the eye and emitted a grand pronouncement: "If God thinks he can pacify me with a box of oranges and grapefruit, he's got another thought coming." With that I flounced upstairs.

Being of a dramatic turn, I am always inclined to end a disagreement with some kind of significant exit, either verbal or physical. However, in the past these usually turned their mocking faces on me, revealing me to be, not tragic as I had intended, but comic. I remember the time I put the coup on a heated discussion by gathering myself up grandly from the table in a final flurry, seeking to put a magnificent touch to this disagreeable conversation—and banged my knee painfully on the table corner. This caused me to react in an agony of reflex and, consequently, to knock over my chair and quickly clutch for it, setting the water glass tipping over on the linen cloth—a picture of classic comedy.

So this morning I flounced rather cautiously, remembering another time when I ended an argument with David by exiting dramatically from the room, having had, of course, the last word. Suddenly I had hit a slick spot on the highly waxed hallway floor, which landed me most ingloriously flat on my face, an epitome of the ridiculous.

The fires within me had been dampened, however, and it wasn't long after I reached my room that I began to be overwhelmed. These fruits were like an appeasement offering! Oh, I knew they had been sent by friends, but the timing of their arrival was of God. It was as though he were saying, "I know you're worn out and weary. With good reason, I might say. Go ahead. Get it out of your system. Here's just a little bit of sunshine from Florida to tide you over. And by the way, I hope you'll see the humor in this little stroke of genius."

Tears began to stream down my cheeks. An appeasement offering—to think that the Everlasting Father of the Universe would care enough to bend close to an obnoxious female creation, and would not be offended by her presumptuous temper tantrums. How could he love me so? I had misbehaved badly. Didn't he strike people dead or with ghastly diseases when they shook their rebellious fists in his face? No, it seems as though he often condescends to touch our lives when we are acting our very worst.

I remembered the words of a Christian counselor from my high school days, "God doesn't expect any more from you than you are able to give as a high schooler." Maybe God didn't expect any more from me than what a young mother with small children—trying to find her own identity while being a pastor's wife, muddling through the self-authentication process that normally occurs in the twenties—could possibly give!

At any rate, the appeasement offering forced me to learn the meaning of anger and of how to use it.

My angry morning had not been so much a case of rebellion
as it was an over-vociferous display of true emotional
need. Pressed, my will would have still responded that it
believed in God's goodness. God often responds more
severely when it is the will that is rebelling. This incident
taught me that an honest reaction of feelings is a matter
of another kind. I have learned that God is never offended by
honest emotions.

How many times he refused to respond to my prayer
requests, often for weeks or months. Then when I finally spilled
forth my anguished frustrations, suddenly the heavens
opened and he overwhelmed me with his love. He was not
attempting to teach me that he only waits until I'm angry to
act, but to show me the importance of truth and the true
knowing of myself. He had waited until my anger became a
catalyst for honesty.

I love the Psalms because they are honest expressions of
emotions. We must be careful not to interpret them as
doctrinal dissertations so much as poignant journals of a soul
bared before God. For instance, King David's cry in Psalm 109
is against those who have acted wickedly, and as far as I
can detect, they are the musings of an angry man:

May his days be few;
*   may another seize his goods!*
May his children be fatherless,
*   and his wife a widow!*
May his children wander about and beg;
*   may they be driven out of the ruins they inhabit!*
May the creditor seize all that he has;
*   may strangers plunder the fruits of his toil!*
Let there be none to extend kindness to him,
*   nor any to pity his fatherless children!*

This theme continues for another eight verses! It is not so
much the attitude which we should seek to emulate—in fact,
Christ tells us we are to bless our enemies, bless and
curse not—but it is the honesty of expression before God that
we should learn to model.

Emotional maturity is the ability to know what it is that I am

feeling, what its name is, then to discover positive channels
for it. The quicker the process operates in us, the more
mature we are becoming. Spiritual emotional maturity
requires that we submit to this procedure before the Lord.
Psalm 4 has an intriguing injunction on this subject.
Verse 4 says, "Be angry, but sin not; commune with your own
hearts on your beds, and be silent."

I think this is the perfect pattern to emulate when dealing
with the emotion of anger. The Scripture does not say
that anger is sin. In fact, it tells us to be angry but sin not. In
other words, it is not the emotion, but rather what we do
with the emotion that can become sin. "Commune with your
own hearts on your beds, and be silent." Come to terms with
what has caused this emotion and be still until you understand
it and have considered the options of handling it.

So I am angry this morning. I can bang pots and pans and
snarl at my loved ones, or I can arrest myself in a moment,
detach that intellectual part of me which is able to function
apart from the emotional, and I can evaluate, "How
surprising! I'm in a rage again this day! What has caused it?
And what are my choices now in the use of this surging,
excess, unasked-for emotion?"

The options are always multiple. I can continue storming
and foaming, I can dump the internal boiling kettle on the
innocent (or maybe not-so-innocent). I can suppress it and
allow myself to be filled with self-pity which eventually
accumulates into dark thunderclouds. I can chew and gnaw at
this unseemly thing, brooding over it until I finally
come to love it, or I can refuse these negative channels and
find positive conduits for this surging strength.

"Let all bitterness and wrath and anger and clamor and
slander be put away from you, with all malice..." says the
writer of Ephesians. These are the results of anger when
the chosen options have been negative ones. A few verses
before this we are told again, "Be angry but do not sin; do not
let the sun go down on your anger, and give no opportunity
to the devil."

Yes, countless creative possibilities spread before me,
positive ways to handle this strong emotion, ways to say,
"I am angry," without sinning. One distressed summer before

the birth of our fourth child, I used my emotion to motivate me to organize the entire house. "I'm tired of things always being in disorder! of never having a place for everything and nothing ever being in its place!"

When we were criticized for taking into our home a person with a fragmented personality, I poured forth my indignation by hammering on the typewriter. The result was a prize-winning allegory about the household of God and those who stand without its gates waiting for an invitation to come in. A flash of rage would often clarify issues for me which before had been dim and foggy. I learned I could be angry without sin!

In time I became well acquainted with my own anger and discovered that it came less often. As I learned to identify it, determine its source, then find an outlet, deep rage came less and less to me. I had handled the cumulative debts; now only current bills needed payment.

I learned always to use anger but never to allow it to use me. The example of Jesus cleansing the Temple is often cited as a case for righteous indignation, and that it is; but let us never make the error of thinking that Christ had gone out of control. No, he was spiritually and emotionally mature. To have lost control would have been sin, and he knew no sin. Our Lord understood completely the nature of his indignation and what best to do with it. He was in charge of it; it was not in charge of him.

Thus, on one angry morning in my life, a love offering was given. He left the fruits of the field, the products of the sun, at the stormy portals of a raging woman-child. Heaven must have enjoyed the Creator laughing beyond the time of that earth-bound February day. And I began to come to terms with One who knows all there is to know about angry mornings, for he has had quite a few himself: "Therefore the anger of the Lord was kindled against his people, and he stretched out his hand against them and smote them."

But not against me on this day—that is the wonder of it—not against me. Blessing was poured out instead. Blessing and laughter—and I began to be irrevocably altered because of his good gifts.

EIGHT
NIGHT TERRORS, DAY ARROWS

He who dwells in the shelter of the Most High,
who abides in the shadow of the Almighty,
will say to the Lord, "My refuge and my fortress;
my God, in whom I trust.

For he will deliver you from the snare of the fowler
and from the deadly pestilence;
he will cover you with his pinions,
and under his wings you will find refuge;
his faithfulness is a shield and buckler.

You will not fear the terror of the night,
nor the arrow that flies by day,
nor the pestilence that stalks in darkness,
nor the destruction that wastes at noonday.

A thousand may fall at your side,
ten thousand at your right hand;
but it will not come near you.

Psalm 91

Soon after we moved into the apartment in the city, Randy's nightmares began. Three, four times a night, I would be wrenched awake by his screams of terror. My response became so conditioned that I often found myself out of bed at the first child-whimper, even before waking. David was a sound sleeper, and I reasoned that since *I* could often grab a nap in the afternoon, and his work schedule was extremely heavy, he should not be disturbed. So this became a fight for us to fight alone, my son and I.

He thrashed in fright, crying, screaming—yet nothing I did seemed to subdue his terror. Holding him tightly, shaking him, walking with him, bringing him drinks, calling his name, all were of no avail. For short but awful periods my child seemed to be drawn into nightmares from which there was no awakening. For fifteen minutes, or twenty, we wrestled with the unknown. "What do you see?" I would question, hoping for some clue, but he could only pant and shrug his shoulders at the thought of revealing the bedside intruders.

Our pediatrician casually informed me that many children his age experience nightmares which they soon outgrow. But nightmares once or twice a week, to another mother, and nightmares two or three times a night, to *me*, were completely different matters. I dragged through the days because of interrupted sleep and finally snuggled down to bed with one ear cocked in readiness to lend futile assistance to my embattled boy. Patiently, I waited for these evening agonies to be outgrown, but they seemed only to increase.

We attempted to provide a daily environment that would not harass the night. Saturday morning cartoons on television were prohibited, and strictures were placed against reading friends' comics. We struggled to give all the children quality time, and to discover soothing mendicants against this one's intense personality—quiet play before bedtime, long opportunities to be alone in our children's communal nursery, unhurried talks in which hidden fears could be expressed. Yet the nightmares went on.

One night before I pulled the covers up to his little chin, I prayed over him: "Dear Jesus, you know that Randy has nightmares. We are asking you to fill his dreams with the beauties of the day, of ponies for riding, butterflies for chasing, and friends to laugh with; of Grandpa's farm, the muddy creek for wading, the cows in the pasture, and the shed roof for climbing. Help these good things to so flood his mind that there will be no room for the bad." He slept peacefully.

"A coincidence," I reasoned. Perhaps the outgrowing had begun. Consequently, I seesawed during the following year in my application of this prayer.

Once, in torment, he came to my bed, a frightened little rag-tag visitor. He lay on the floor, my pillow beneath his head, with his eyes wide open against the shadows of the room. Holding his sweaty fist, too weary myself to pronounce the words of prayer, I suggested that we chant in unison the name of Jesus. Over and over we repeated, "Jesus... Jesus... Jesus..." Shortly, we were both asleep, hands joined awkwardly over the side of the bed.

Finally, I had to admit that it did seem as though there were either no nightmares—or at least fewer—on the nights I remembered to pray for protection before Randy went to sleep. Sometimes dishes or company or other children were a more immediate demand in the light than the terrors we could possibly face in the coming dark. But each time we prayed, it did seem as though my commending the love of God to fill his trembling body soothed both of us and brought quick calm.

At any rate, it didn't matter if I vacillated between conviction and question, Randy had become absolute. "Pray with me," he would demand each night before sleep; and if awakened by the terror of the dark, he would come to my bedside, no longer just for my presence, but for my prayers.

After four years of living in the middle of the city, we moved to one of Chicago's next-door suburbs. From the first night there, he slept soundly. The outgrowing had finally come. It had been instantaneous, concurrent with a geographical relocation, and there were no relapses. Like mothers everywhere, I "pondered these things in my heart." The ritual of bedtime prayers was maintained, but there no longer seemed to be a need for special prayers of protection. We had faced the terror and seemingly conquered. The arrow that flies by day, however, was something new with which to contend.

One afternoon I noticed Randy squinting with a distressed expression on his face. "What are you looking at?" I demanded.

"All the little things," he replied.

"What little things?" I wondered. "Maybe if you stopped squinting your eyes, you would see things as they really are."

He looked up at me, his face still contorted. "No, it's when I open my eyes that I see them. They're little things like people walking. I'm squinting so I won't see them."

He had started seeing these earlier, on a vacation trip with my parents. "Well, did you tell Dobie [Grandma] that you saw them?" I investigated.

"Yes," he replied, still squinting. "But she saw them too." I laughed, overwhelmed by my mother's active and sometimes not-too-helpful imagination.

He didn't like seeing what he saw; sometimes there were skulls or ugly faces, but most often "little things walking like people." Trying to handle this casually and hoping it too would pass, we would pray and then I would send him off to active, not passive, pursuits.

Several months after this began, a young couple came to my husband with an apology. They had come to dinner without telling us that they were just wearing off the effects of an LSD dosage "dropped" that afternoon. Looking back, I realized they had been a little quiet, but there had been many at our round table, and the laughter and conversation had camouflaged their silence. Considering their state, I thought they had conducted themselves remarkably well. "The trip was wearing off by dinnertime," they explained, although they were still "seeing things" now and then on the dining room wall.

I had a rush of alarm. Randy's vivid imaginings had begun about the same time—could he possibly have been moderately hallucinating? Could a miniscule gram of the acid been left on a goblet? Could he have sipped a drink from the unwashed glass?

Questioning our church's resident drug expert—there were several; this particular young man had found Christ in a jail in Italy after being imprisoned for smuggling hashish—I was startled by his reply. "I doubt it," he answered thoughtfully. "But there might have been an accompanying demon."

He went on to relate several incidents when he had opened himself to the power of the enemy through the use of drugs.

By chance that same week, I spent some time with a veteran

missionary from New Guinea. She began to relate experiences of spiritual warfare and remarked how unprepared new missionaries often were to do battle with a real foe. She lamented that mission boards sometimes neglect to train these workers to use the necessary weapons for this kind of combat. "Often their children suffer the most," she explained. "They'll suddenly begin to have tremendous nightmares." My heart leaped. "Often several a night from which they wake up screaming and in terror."

"What would you tell them to do in the face of this?" I inquired. "Something very simple," she responded—she was obviously a seasoned pro. "I'd have the parents lay hands on that child and in the name of Jesus Christ and through the enabling power of his blood, refuse the power of the enemy to disturb."

Insight dawned; I knew what it was all about. Perhaps I had instinctively realized it for years. No human being had taught me how to deal with the foul methods of One who could keep a city in his stronghold, who would stoop to torment a babe in the hopes of short-circuiting the parents' ministry. We had intruded into forbidden chambers, hoping to bring light and love. We were to pay for our audacity.

Yet, something had tutored me, something had called out my natural mother's instincts. Something whispered to me—though I was admittedly slow to hear—about the powerful potion of prayer. Though I was absolutely ignorant about war maneuvers, something gave me knowledge, enabled me through my intuition to protect my own.

Whereas the night terrors had taken four years to vanquish, the day arrows called for immediate front-line confrontation. This time I knew what was about—foul play. Each night, I went to the child's bed, unasked, and laid hands on the sleeping form. I silently refused the power of the enemy through the name of Jesus Christ and the power of his blood. The squinting soon ceased.

Those were my raw recruit days. Now, major battles later, some on behalf of myself, some for others, I too am becoming a veteran of spiritual warfare. I have ceased to be afraid when I sense that battle lines are forming. I have seen my adversary turn tail and retreat too many times to run any longer in fear. Wariness, however, is often in order, since I know something of the depths of his deviousness—and I watch my chicks like a mother hawk, keeping sentry until I am sure all is secure.

I have discovered certain general principles on the deployment of troops to be almost fail-safe. The first is: Take quick, incisive action the moment you realize you are being approached by enemy forces. Mobilize immediately into counterattack. Don't delay, and above all, don't discuss terms with your adversary. The best way to gain the offensive is to sound a battle cry.

"Man shall not live by bread alone, but by every word that proceeds from the mouth of God," was the quiet alarm sounded by Christ when met by the tempter in the wilderness. No discussion here, no dallying, just one incisive thrust with the Sword of the Spirit, that Word of God which is alive and powerful.

Second, having overpowered supernatural evil, express gratitude for the victory, but don't concentrate on it. Too many Christians are like old soldiers, ruminating endlessly on tales of past victory, but missing the ongoing work of God, the overall battle strategy.

"Lord, even the demons are subject to us in your name!" was the amazed reaction of the disciples to the results of their first spiritual skirmishes. Christ's ready reply is extremely interesting: "I saw Satan fall like lightning from heaven. Behold, I have given you authority to tread upon serpents and scorpions, and over all the power of the enemy; and nothing shall hurt you. Nevertheless do not rejoice in this, that the spirits are subject to you; but rejoice that your names are written in heaven" (Luke 10:17-20).

Our Lord was well aware how easily we humans become fascinated with supernatural evil. We delight in witch hunts. Our minds all too quickly gravitate to what is bad, instead of holding to and affirming what is good. But Christ gives us advice like this: "Yes, Satan exists, and you have authority over him. But don't even bother to give him the time of day. Concentrate your attention on God's works of grace."

The reason for this, I believe, is that Satan delights when we concentrate on evil, when we dwell on the negative, when we deliberate on our own flaws or the flaws of others. His subterfuge is to lead us into a reverse idolatry. In reality, many of us come close to worshiping what is evil, and when we concentrate on the demons in ourselves or others, *we call them out. We free them.*

"Rejoice that your names are written in heaven," said Christ. *When we concentrate on the good, we call it out—in ourselves, in one another. We free it.*

I've also learned that the way we conduct mopping-up operations is as important as the way we carry on the conflict. Satan would like to foul us up at any point.

Third, always expect the presence of supernatural good. The Heavenly Hosts are in command of the field charts. Like wise generals, they remain inactive tacticians as long as I am holding my own. But the moment I falter and *remember* to sound the bugle for help, Someone is soon by my side hacking away with me, offering a shield for my defense. My depleted strength is renewed; I become a war maiden, wielding a singing sword above my head—and the enemy is often afraid of me.

I'm grateful for the terror of the night, for screams and clammy little handholds. I'm grateful for the arrows of the day, imagined skulls, shadows against the walls, and squinted faces. So learned one child the elements of spiritual battle; so learned one ignorant mother. I'm grateful for the promise of the Word, for the power of Christ's name, and his blood, poured somehow, mysteriously, into time. I know that though a thousand fall at our side, ten thousand at our right hand, they shall not come near us.

NINE
MISOGYNIST

mi sog y nist n. [see MISOGNY], a person, especially a man, who hates women.—*Webster's New World Dictionary*

"We'd love to come," said the voice on the other end of the receiver, "but only if we don't sit around and talk about babies all evening."

I was shocked. Not that the words had been spoken, but that they were directed at me! How often had I inwardly cherished the exact thoughts.

Women's gatherings always seemed to end in tedious conversations on limited topics: my possessions, or my man. Young marrieds could be even worse, describing endlessly three life events: 1. The details of bearing and/or breastfeeding babies; 2. The disciplining of children, particularly potty training; 3. The mother game—i.e., my child is better than your child, he/she learns/grows faster, longer, sooner, prettier, smarter, higher, sweeter.

My ire began to rise as I hung the phone in its cradle. She couldn't possibly have meant me. I prided myself on my conversational arts. I didn't even carry photos of the children in my wallet, to prevent myself from boring people. Yet how discomforting my own pet thoughts sounded when spoken aloud! How uncharitable they seemed. How superior. How self-satisfied.

Although I had never verbalized those thoughts except in
tearful, frustrated privacy to my husband, after a women's
meeting which had dragged on in endless tedium (with
older women bragging on their *grandchildren* being faster,
smarter, better, etc.), I had declared the same thought in
another subtle way. Often I explained that I preferred
the company of my husband's friends—"men make more
interesting conversation."

*"We'd love to come, but only if we don't sit around and talk about
babies all evening."* How often have I thought the same thing?
Then why the anger, why the indignation toward this
woman? Was it because she didn't have children and was
presuming I was that sort of mother? Or was it because hearing
the words spoken by another voice allowed me to identify
in myself a deeply planted misogynism, a hatred of my own
sex? Wasn't there creeping intolerance in those words, and
wasn't I guilty of the same feeling of intellectual superiority?

But from where did this misogynism come? From my father
who bought me a tractor when I was five, and also insisted
I think and develop my verbal skills in hot debate? No, that
was not the source. What about my mother with her keen
enjoyment of me as a feminine mirror of herself, and her
amazingly wide circle of accomplished women friends?
Neither was she to blame. What was the source of this ghastly
snobbery, this inclination to disapproval, this harsh judgment
on the woman part of me?

How much had another family influenced me, the family
of the godly? Had the Christian subculture unconsciously
offered me a drink laced with poison, and had I accepted the
cup of interpreted doctrine, subtly loaded with latent,
though unstated, misogynism?

Was there another part of me lurking in some buried grotto?
Was I refusing her the light, this shadow side of me, because
she was unlike the other women around me, those who
were approved, acceptable. Did I fear that if I allowed her to be
recognized, she would be ostracized?

What was this unidentified fear I felt in the company of
committed Christians, those who had never treated me with
anything but love? Why did I cower as though waiting

for a blow, cringe because I sensed I might do something wrong?

What was I doing to this hidden part of me, was I subordinating it, making it a changeling? Certainly it too had been created by God, this mind-and-idea side of me, constantly doing battle with the more abstract concepts of life. Was I verbalizing the need of *this* side in a subconscious way—by saying I prefer the company of men over women?

Genesis records, "So God created man in his own image, in the image of God he created him; male and female he created them." Perhaps I am both male and female. Perhaps there is a deeper meaning to this verse. Jung maintained that the human was composed of the anima (female) and the animus (male). Perhaps I was suppressing the male part of my woman, that incisive analytical part of me; and in the process I had come to resent the female of my woman. And now this resentfulness was being directed in impatience toward other women.

Who were my friends? I really had no close women friends. Didn't they say if you couldn't be a friend to yourself, you couldn't be a friend to anyone else either? Some grand internal reconciliation needed to be made between my confident, swaggering alter-ego and the other intuitive, easily crushed pearl of myself. Each needed to discover its eminent domain in my soul, to coexist peaceably, to enjoy its own territorial privileges.

Awakening moments can be small or great. This one took only the ring of a phone. Suddenly, my head was awash with insights, many of which I could scarcely handle. I did know that an intolerance toward some part of me had become a fence posted between myself and others, with "NO TRESPASSING" nailed to the gate.

Questions, questions. They followed in rapid succession that afternoon, and few of the answers trailed behind. Yet I knew one thing for certain: I would promise never to say, and attempt not even to think, "We'd love to come, but only if we don't sit around talking about babies all evening."

TEN
FATAL FLAW

I have an Achilles heel, the wound of which, I suppose, will never heal, but can only be stanched. It is my fatal flaw, and it has a tendency to erupt at the most unexpected moments through the seasons of my life, leaving fresh marks on the springs as well as the snows. Through the years it has been somewhat contained, but pain from its reopening is always possible. I have no joy or laughter in revealing this flaw, as I do in sharing other things in my life, and that is how I know the grief of it is still with me.

Perhaps a healing is coming in the days ahead, but I have an intuition that this is my thorn. I suppose I must wear it in order to be able to say, "I know what it is like to have to learn to live with something terrible." There is a victory in that, as well.

This wound bleeds spontaneously, at its own will. It seeps into the creative joints of me, stifling the potential of my art, inhibiting my mothering and wifing.

It is my tendency to look back at life already lived and sigh, "It might have been, it might have been..." It is the remnant echo, the leftover fabric of a cry, "If only I had... If only I hadn't..."

It has haunted me since birth, at least since early memory, and I suspect it is a genetic sort of thing, some wild eruption in my genes, inherited directly from neither parent. Some chromosome in me is twisted, ill-formed, causing me to carry the dreadful potential of never fulfilling the purpose for which God created me. It is my tragic possibility, the strong pulling on the inside of me that will keep me from making any significant contributions.

In high school I was secretary of my senior class. I was assigned the simple task of writing to a cap and gown company and ordering over three hundred of each for graduation, a certain number royal blue and a certain number white. Along with this I was to write and order the diplomas.

I delayed and delayed while the last year of high school stretched into winter, and winter began to turn in its season as well. I delayed, though reminded countless times by our class sponsor. Finally, in exasperation and irritation, he asked if I had sent those letters—and I lied and said that I had. My lie was heard by a close friend who later accused me: "Karen, you lied!" She was amazed, but I was more so.

Rushing home after school, I wrote and mailed the letters so my lie would not be so profound. Several weeks later our class sponsor had another few words with me.

"You sent those letters to the diploma and cap and gown companies, didn't you?"

"Oh, yes," I responded brightly, relieved that I could say the words without staining my soul.

"Well," he continued. "You took so much time that I finally asked the class vice-president to write the letters, which she did. It's a good thing I took those precautions, because your correspondence has been returned. You sent the order for the diplomas to the cap and gown company, and the order for the caps and gowns to the diploma company."

Some people might laugh at this, but even now I can't find it in my heart to force a smile. The telling of it, even some twenty years later, is still extremely painful.

He continued. "The teachers have had you on quite a pedestal around here. I think it's time they took Karen Burton off of it."

The horror and shame of this incident for me was not in the fact that he thought I should be taken off the pedestal. I have always hated pedestals. They can be a subtle form of idolatry. It is not for nothing that we are told, "Thou shalt

make no image before thee." When we make another
human an image we conform him to our expectation of what
he should be, and then we adore it. There is only one way
to go from a pedestal, and that is to descend. So losing
my position was, if anything, a relief.

No, I was distressed because of the terrible realization that
my whole senior class, some three hundred students, would
have had to march through graduation without their caps and
gowns, only to receive no diplomas, all because of me.
I discovered that my flaw within had the potential to bring
grief not only to myself but to the lives of others around me.

*I know that God allowed this painful incident in my life, and I
suspect that it is he who refuses to heal me from the shame
of its memory. He needed to impress me with the ever-present,
awful whisper of disaster.*

All the early years of my marriage were shadowed by the
possibility of this wound opening and spurting over the bright
promise of our life. "Have you called so-and-so?" my efficient
husband has had to ask thousands of times over. [Have
you written the letters for your graduating class yet?]
"Did you make that appointment?" [We will have to take you
off the pedestal.] "When are you going to get together
with that person, as you promised?" [Two by two they march
without their caps and gowns and diplomas.]

It is more than procrastination, more than lack of discipline,
although those are the words I have used to describe it.
There is a deadly whirlpool within me that sucks continually,
seeking to drown me in its vortex. No use blaming it on
my enemy, though he never hesitates to use it against me—no,
this springs from the seed of myself. This is a flaw of my
own nature, my very own. (When are you going to, when are
you going to, when are you going... ?)

I have pulled against it, found the strength to fight it over
each inch of the battleground that has become my life.
Housekeeping and article deadlines, meal preparations for
company and correspondence, loving notes and book reports,
prayer and worship, homework and piano lessons—all of
them, large and small, have been hampered by the bleeding of
my wound.

I am winning more and more of the battles, but the war still rages; my essential nature has not been transformed. Somewhere this thing lurks, with the potential to humiliate me; to cripple me so that I might not carry life into the deadness of others' souls—to those with wounds of their own; to silence me from the singing of word-songs only I can sing.

I am learning to live with this flaw, and I have a vivid memory of the past, of a high-schooler faced with the awful realization of what she was and the potential for pain her flaw might have in her life. It is a memory which does not dim or fade. It was God's word to me saying, "Achilles wounds do not heal. They can only be stanched. Beware."

ELEVEN
THE MOST BEAUTIFUL BABY...

When our first child was brought to my side, I looked at the still-bloody body, a blue hematoma rising on the back of the sausage-like head, the face contorted and squalling, and thought, *this is the most beautiful infant I have ever seen.*

David viewed the same squirming body, the same elongated head, the same wrinkled face and was convinced for the next three days that his firstborn was retarded.

"Did you see the baby?" I remember asking in an euphoric haze as I was being wheeled down the hall. I attributed the somewhat choked nod to my husband's being overcome with the emotions of fathering. "Isn't he beautiful?" I gushed. Another silent shake of the head.

Childbirth has helped me to learn to participate in life's ongoing panorama. During pregnancy something mysteriously godly and awesome is occurring in a woman's body. She instinctively turns inward, listening to that life within. She feels, knowing her awe to be ridiculous, as though this has never happened to anyone before. At the same time, she is keenly aware that it is an incident out of the millions.

Each new child has evoked the same response from me: *Oh! This one is the most beautiful I have ever seen!* It was not until the third time around that childbirth began to take on historic significance.

Perhaps it was because that pregnancy was so filled with fear. My grandmother had died during pregnancy at my age, leaving a boy and girl exactly the ages of mine. And some minor bug I had picked up in South America kept fouling up my blood tests and blotching my skin. My nights were tormented with dreams of death, dreams of retardation, dreams of a woman I had never known. Thinking about the agony of labor brought dread. Could life possibly give us *three* healthy children? Hadn't my aunt, daughter of that very grandmother, died herself in a tragic accident, leaving small children, a girl and a boy? Didn't history repeat itself, like a gyroscope maintaining its own level?

Despite my continued dedication of this unborn child to the will of its Heavenly Father, I had to face each fear again and again over those nine months. In spite of fears, or perhaps because of them, I requested no anesthesia for delivery, and with wild-eyed clarity was able to declare again, *this baby, this moment, this instant of life-giving is the most beautiful I have ever seen.*

Then with the bright labor lights spotlighting my shaking legs and my exhausted "just-push-one-more-time" body, something happened which I knew was due neither to drugs or gas, as I had been administered none. Perhaps it was birthshock, but I seemed so perfectly clear headed.

I could imagine a murmur being whispered throughout the ages beyond and before me. Back, back it was passed to those before—my mother, the grandmothers, one who had died while I had lived, the great-grandmothers. Back it stretched to all women who had shared in these pain-filled rigors, to those who endured tortured labor hour after hour, then had to return to exertions of plowing and planting. *This child, this baby . . .*

I thought of those who had died needlessly of sepsis, death carried on the infected, unwashed hands of examining doctors who had just come from the mortuaries; of Mary who brought forth a man-child, who laid mortal infinity on the hay-prickled manger; of Hannah and Rachel and Sarah, sanctified in their mournful barrenness; and back to Eve who was deceived and brought upon us all this painful reminder of alienation, along with its joyful promise of ultimate, whole new life. They had all whispered in some way or another, *this child, this time, this life-giving is the most beautiful I have ever seen.*

Somehow, the thought ennobled me. By the time that infant had been lifted from my arms, I understood a little about common denominators. Tolerance eased itself around me like a sigh, and I discovered what it meant to be at home as a woman among other women.

How easily we could lose ourselves in the arrested wonder of this moment! I even understood those who abandoned personhood to the cherishing and caring of babies.

Despite all my efforts to be casual, to take the birth events in my life in stride, my soul suddenly knew it was a moment for awesome hushedness—pregnant with life, a realization of a bit of God in each of us. For a moment we as women especially reflect God's image, as creator, life cherisher, sustainer. Our lives are irrevocably altered; we are never more the same. This child, this baby, will be carried in our hearts all our days, and, I suppose, that nurturing, too, is God-like.

"Yet, woman will be saved through bearing children..." I have no idea what Paul meant doctrinally by these words. I only know that, panting with awe on that delivery table, something began to be reconciled in me. I too was part of the life-murmur—*this child, this time*—and it was perfectly natural for me to feel at ease. I had said, "Yes," to the women surrounding me, to those of history, and of today, and to those in the unborn beyond. I had stretched out my arms behind and around and before, and they had stretched out their arms to me. He certainly was the most beautiful baby I had ever seen.

TWELVE
ON TURNING THIRTY

The approaching age of thirty was for me an opportunity for intense soul-scrutiny. It was an innate passage of life built in by the Creator to provide me with moments of truth. I looked deep and I was terrified by what I saw!

The terror was due not to the process of aging—I had always felt too young, and thus welcomed the maturity. No, my panic was because this new decade had advanced upon me so rapidly. Only yesterday I was a bride of eighteen and now, soon, one morning I would awake and be middle-aged! Greatly discontented, I discovered that I was doing all the unimportant things in my life and none of the important.

What's more, I was pregnant again, unexpectedly. I had been pacifying myself with, "When the children are all in school, then I'll start becoming a person of prayer; then I'll have time to master the Scriptures; then I'll begin to write seriously..." Now I could see it would take another six or seven years before I experienced serious growth, if I continued to follow that same line of rationalization.

Something very familiar lurked in the hidden recesses of me. A suspicion began to grow. These first thirty years had gone so fast—couldn't I conceivably pass through the next thirty only to discover myself saying, "Well, when the children are through college, after we have paid off the mortgage on the house, when we retire, then..." Was the fatal flaw again at work in me?

I knew I wasn't what I should be spiritually. The

comparisons between the Christian disciplines in my life and those in the life of my husband were telling. In our family, we regularly run into David poring over his Scriptures, or rush into his study for a pencil or a book, only to interrupt him in prayer. "What are you doing, Daddy?" is regularly answered with, "I'm praying. I'll be done in a little while." (He used to pray on his knees until the skating incident, when I insisted he take some exercise with us in the crisp winter weather. Wobbling, he fell, hit his knee, and sustained some kind of minor but permanent injury which forced him to pace and pray for the next few years!) At any rate, I was not a person of prayer. I rarely spent time with my Bible. I was not using my spiritual gift.

Even as a child I sensed that my ability to write was a gift from God. In junior high an English teacher scribbled across the top of one of my compositions: "Karen, you have the gift of writing. I feel sorry for you. You will be unhappy all your life if you are unable to use it."

In college I validated the freshman writing courses and proceeded into advanced classes, only to discover to my amazement that I had nothing about which to write. The resulting mediocre grades were terribly discouraging, and I suppose I might not have written again except for the fact that, in desperation, I submitted something I had composed at age thirteen. Without corrections, it received an A! I had sense enough to realize that a paper out of the head of a thirteen-year-old which could hold its own in a class of twenty-year-olds indicated a talent given by a Master to be used at his choosing, a gift entrusted.

I was not doing anything I felt I should be doing, none of the important things. I was no closer to seeing them realized in my life at thirty than I had been when I launched into my twenties.

Our church at that time was organized into small cells, based on geographic location, that met for the purpose of prayer. Through regular cell-group meetings, we developed a closeness that encouraged honest sharing of needs. I requested my group to intercede with the Lord for me for three qualities I felt I desperately needed: 1. Discipline 2. Motivation 3. Physical strength.

Mine was the classic case of the tyranny of the urgent.

Because I was undisciplined, my time was dominated by the piles of things needing to be done. I would spend a week absorbed in unstructured reading—anything I could get my hands on, stacks of interesting titles from the library—but then mounds of unwashed laundry would determine the order of the next couple of days. I began creative projects on an emotional impulse; but when the impulse died, they languished. Sewing, reupholstery, stripping antique furniture, poetry—all waited until I caught the inspiration again.

Without motivation it was impossible for me to start such things as cleaning cupboards—or prayer. I would have to wait until things were unbearable, until I was stimulated by guilt, or inspired by a sermon!

Physically, I was haunted by exhaustion. Perhaps three small children had something to do with it, but I have also learned that there usually is a source for such chronic depletion of strength. My emotional energies were as undisciplined as the rest of my life. I would expend them on unnecessary commodities, fritter them away in costly and frivolous adventures—and then have no resources to draw upon when I needed them for the things that were really important to me. Without thinking, I would accept responsibility for a dinner for a hundred, never considering whether this was a wise investment of my time and emotion, or if a project of this nature would really advance me toward my goals.

I suspect I was also often physically exhausted because of the misuse of my creativity. My junior high English teacher had indeed been prophetic—I would always be unhappy as long as I denied my chief gift its proper outlet. An artistic ability is a dangerous thing to contain; it is like floodwaters surging behind a dam. Unable to find its natural course, the tide overflows the banks, overwhelming the surrounding lands with its forces. The artist denied is often neurotic. I was to learn that the use of my gift was not only a matter of spiritual obedience—it was essential for my emotional health.

Looking back, I can now see that it was at this passage into the decade of my thirties that the Lord began to answer those several years' worth of prayers. Personally, I am convinced that spiritual growth is stimulated by God. Unless he chooses to draw us, we remain so mired in our humanity that we are powerless to come to him. All these little incidents in my life, these flashes of light, these rare moments of understanding, were gifts from him—maps that eventually led me through previously uncharted and dangerous lands, directly to him. With thirty staring me in the face, he began to give me unusual answers to my requests. He gave me insomnia and an unplanned pregnancy at the passage into my third decade.

I obviously did not fit the role of a typical pastor's wife. Our church during those years was admittedly among the avant-garde of evangelicalism. There were no traditions to bind us, and we were free to experiment. Our congregation was distinctive, to say the least. It was composed largely of young adults out of the sixties who were eager to find alternatives to what they considered the stultifying church experiences of their past. I know I took particular pride in my own iconoclastic contributions, and I did not consider myself different from any other member of the congregation just because I was the minister's wife. The nicest thing anyone said to me during those years was: "You don't look like any pastor's wife I remember!"

With such a casual approach to my role, I was consequently ill-prepared for other people's expectations, and their criticisms when I did not measure up. All leaders, whether preachers or politicians, spend much of their life under the gun. And much of the scatter-shooting spills over to the leader's spouse. Fortunately for me, there could have been no better place to try my wings than Circle Church. We were all renegade in one way or another; it was just that I was a little more outspoken than the rest. Any other congregation would have found me intolerable! At any rate, what criticism I did receive woke me up at night and kept me awake.

Fortunately for my growth, I have always been thin-skinned about criticism. I take it to heart! Not for me the rationalization that the party making the nasty comments was dead wrong; rather, I always assumed that something in what the person said (or in what others told me he had said) just might possibly be true. I always felt it was my duty to examine and discover that element of truth. Though often carried to extreme (sometimes negative comments are way off track), this characteristic in me was a redeeming feature. I have often needed to hear what people had to say about me—in the words of Robert Burns, "Oh wod some power the giftie gie us, to see oursels as others see us!"—even though it caused me grief.

As I tossed those many wakeful nights, the influence of one of the women from my past, my own childhood pastor's wife, reached out to me. I remember Mother mentioning that the only time Mrs. Roberts, with her varied responsibilities and six children, could find time to pray was at three A.M. She regularly rose at this time to meet with God.

Since I was awake anyway, and since I too was a pastor's wife, no matter how reluctantly, and since I knew I should be developing regular habits of prayer (and since I thought this smacked a wee bit of the romantic martyr), I decided I might as well use these wakeful hours positively. I bought a standard size notebook and began to fill the pages. In three years' time, I used a meager seventeen of them.

Scanty, immature thoughts, focused entirely on my own self, my wants and desires—nevertheless, it was a start. Oh the power of prayer, this small wedge driven into my ennui! How precious are the feeble beginnings, and how we need to encourage them in one another! It was here that the supernatural good fixed a toehold.

It was then that I discovered I was pregnant again. I was overwhelmed! It was not the child that was unwanted, it was the caring and sustaining and nurturing of that child which seemed to be beyond my physical abilities. I empathize with all the people who drag through life. An evening of hospitality—and there were hundreds of such evenings—could put me to bed for a couple of days. A stimulating conversation could weary me; a counseling session could drain me. How could I manage four children if I was barely getting by with three?

The average age of our congregation was twenty-seven. Older Christians were in scant supply. I began to be hungry for a maturity that was beyond my peer level. Cautiously, I would sidle up to the few older women I knew and inquire, I hoped not too obviously, "How in the world did you manage to raise your four children?" Most of them were in a bliss of forgetfulness and would mutter, "Oh, somehow we got by." There were none who would give me handholds to keep me from self-destructing in the fast-approaching days ahead.

Obviously, I was going to have to do it myself, and time was at a nine-month premium. Setting my teeth, I realized I would have to come to terms with my mismanagement, and somewhere, from some unknown resource in my soul, I drew on an ability to wake each morning of that pregnancy with unshakable determination. I would organize my life. I would be disciplined. I would be motivated. I would function *in* weariness and *out* of it.

The last unusual answer to my prayers was the oncoming, unstoppable, rolling caissons of thirty. It was as though I had finally reached my unique age of accountability. For me, it was now or never. I was haunted by eschatological possibilities. I could envision myself one day standing before the throne of God for the ultimate examination, and in utter despicability I could hear myself stammering... "But... but... but I never had time to know you, Lord. There were the children you gave me, and there was the redecorating of the houses. There were seasonal fashions to buy and sew, there was my husband to feed. There were mirrors to hang in every room. There were mysteries to read. There was much trivia to attend to—"

"ENOUGH! ENOUGH!" I could imagine those enthronged forces booming, and then all of the universes echoing, "ENOUGH! ENOUGH!"

"You were given time enough!" would come the multivoice from the white throne. "You were given a lifetime. You chose to fritter it away in all the nonessentials! You have put everything before us! You loved them well, and us not at all!"

"No time!" the voice on the right would shout in amazement. "You spent more time serving TV than you did worshiping us."

"No time!" would chime the voice in the middle. "You spent more time researching the history, literature, and philosophy of the early twentieth century in Europe than in seeking our face."

"No time!" would cry the voice on the left. "You spent more time stimulating yourself with shopping than in nourishing yourself with our living water."

Then all the voices at once, the ones around the throne and the ones before it, the ones behind and below and above: "You were given time enough!"

The pronouncement would be given. "Karen Mains nee Burton. Stand forth. To whom much is given, much is required. There are no excuses! None whatsoever are allowed!"

Fanciful? Perhaps, but my dreams at this period of my life had a strangely recurrent theme. I was often back in high school and failing an exam because I had not prepared myself for it. I had not turned in a report or I had lost an assignment. My class was graduating, but there was no diploma for me. My subconscious seemed to be projecting a clear message to my conscious mind.

All these things came together during those nine months of pregnancy. I needed an emotion, any emotion, to stimulate action; anger was my springboard into function. I would carve out of my life the time to be what God wanted me to be. No excuses; none whatsoever. I would learn to clean on schedule, and not at any other time. I would develop systems that would help my household function and also leave me free to develop spiritual growth. Everything was to be in order by 9:30 in the morning—all the routine tasks finished— even if it meant I would have to rise at 4:00! Then I would use the rest of the morning to deplete the mountain of ironing, unclutter the closets, and finish special projects. The afternoons, naptimes, would be used for my own self and, I hoped, for time with God. The rooms were to be picked up each night even if my tongue dragged in exhaustion on the floor!

It was a grim undertaking, grimly undertaken.

However, by the end of those nine months, I who had considered myself the world's greatest softie, if not a physical weakling, had proved to myself that I could do it. My house was organized from top to bottom and I was accomplishing the work in proper order, on schedule. Though I felt I knew the strains of infirmity, age, and obesity all at the same time—the baby, a boy, came two weeks late and weighed 10 lbs. 15 oz.—and I had kept on with my goal!

It was true, only a few books had been read, no lovely trips to the Art Institute had been planned, a minimal amount of hospitality had gone on in our home. I had not even attended church for the last three months, because of my ungainliness—but I knew I could do it! I could keep a house functioning without the impetus of company coming. I could clean on a schedule and have free hours in the afternoon!

Hey, you cloud of witnesses! Look at me! Have you been cheering me on from your observation posts in the grandstands? Look at me! Oh, I know it's not a major accomplishment, as spiritual victories go. It's not like facing a pride of famished lions with disdainful confidence. It's not blithely skipping into the fiery furnace. It's not marching to the stake with a hymn in one's throat—but oh, for me, for me it's huge. Are you hurrahing me? Are you shouting, "Run, run the race"? Are you chanting, "Go! Go!! GO!!!"

The Lord did a lovely thing for me after that terrible three-quarters of a year of struggle. He gave me a retreat in my hospital room, and even a view. Lake Michigan scudded and foamed in her December garments outside. I watched with placid smugness as medical students scurried frantically across the courtyards and pavements eight floors below.

No one came to occupy the bed on the other side of my long room—in fact, the whole maternity ward was exceptionally quiet. There was just the wonderful, wonderful silence and the serene feeling of all my jobs done—and my new *Living Bible.*

Uninterrupted, I began to devour those pages. Overfed in my past, in recent years I had found the Scriptures lifeless, old, and overused. Suddenly, with this frank and ungarnished paraphrase, they became fresh and delightful.

"What are you laughing about?" queried a startled nurse, poking her head into my room at 3:00 in the morning.

"Oh, I couldn't sleep and I was just reading," I answered, hiding the book underneath the sheets.

"What are you reading, dearie?" she probed.

"The Bible," I replied, smiling.

Little toeholds in my life had been made, spiritual

grappling-hooks which would open the path by which he would tread into my soul. The Word had come to me in recognizable—and some scarcely recognizable—ways, but it had come. The tiny stirrings I began to feel in that hospital room would eventually grow into an intense hunger that nothing would be able to sate, apart from the eventual mysterious imparting of his Presence unto me.

Unaware of all of this at that time, I enjoyed the quiet, read my new Bible, and had the great contentment of knowing that I would hit thirty with colors flying.

THIRTEEN
A DIALOG

Young Mother:	Lord! Lord, are you listening?
Lord:	Yes, I am here.
Young Mother:	Lord, where are the older women who will "Titus" me?
Lord:	Just exactly what did you have in mind?
Young Mother:	How am I to manage four children—this next one due unexpectedly—a house, a husband in the ministry, people in the church who look to me for guidance, two mother cats which have just had nine kittens between them and have become insanely jealous, a hyperactive phone, guests coming and going for breakfast, lunch, and dinner, and after and in-between? How am I to manage and not lose my way as a person, to become who you want me to be, and still be a responsible steward of the personal gifts you have given me?
Lord:	Again, what did you have in mind?

Young
Mother: A woman. An older woman. Someone who has read Titus 2:3, 4, and 5. Someone who realizes she has a scriptural mandate to teach me how to be sensible, chaste, domestic, kind, and submissive. Someone who will teach what is good. Lord, where are the older women who will Titus me?

Lord: Dear child, didn't you know? They've all gone to work.

FOURTEEN
"I WANT TO WRITE!"

"I will not throw the bust of Shakespeare," I vowed. David had given it to me years before as an anniversary present. *I will not throw anything. Throwing things is an immature, senseless way of expressing anger.*

A shopping excursion had taken me from home for a few hours, and now I was paying for it. A mother always pays for release-time from housework. My pleasant luncheons planned for the very purpose of getting-away-from-it-all were always spoiled when I returned to the ruins. Although the house hadn't been immaculate when I left, it had been an hour away from the verge of being clean. Now it would take the better part of the evening to repair.

Under control, I gave Will Shakespeare's bald pate a pat and waded through tinker toys and puzzles to survey the devastation in the kitchen. *That was too much.*

Spilled sugar and flavored punch mix gummed in a pinkish mess on the floor. Sticky forks and spoons, haphazard dishes, and an entire cupboard emptied of glasses, each sitting half full, assaulted my only recently calmed sensibilities. A baby food jar of pureed spinach was handily within reach on the high chair. I winged it with all my might against the upper right-hand corner of the farthest cupboard of the kitchen, marched upstairs, slammed the door, flung myself on the bed, and waited for the inclination to destroy to pass.

My children still talk about "the time Mommy threw the jar of spinach." Maybe that is because for once they had to clean up after me! I certainly demonstrated to them the scientific principle of ejection. The projectile sailed one way, but the contents of the projectile splattered a creamy green slime in the opposite direction—onto the dining room carpet, the stuccoed wall, the mirror over the buffet. I found dried spinach on the doorway months later.

Through the years I have succumbed to this inclination to throw things. Three pans with craggy stumps in place of handles hide in the cupboard and are awkward to use during meal preparation. I keep them to remind me of useless passion.

The first was tossed during year two of our marriage, when my husband invited last-minute company, people I had never met, much less had the chance to learn to love. It was not the invitation that was really the problem, though, it was the circumstances. The baby was fussing, there wasn't enough food, and the minutes were marching in double time across the kitchen clock—all demands I hadn't yet developed the stamina to cope with. I had winged the pan against the counter and watched it bang one way while the handle bounced another. In cool dismay I thought, "This is rather an expensive way to vent emotion."

So goes the tale of the saucepan. The skillet, however, went flying during a two-year-old's marathon temper tantrum which was going on its second hour. I guess I thought it was legal for Mommy to have a temper tantrum too. The third pan I can't remember throwing, although the odds were that I was probably fuming over something done by my husband.

To be fair to myself, I feel compelled to make it clear that I never threw these items *at anyone*, only in empty rooms laden with my own tension.

Reaction to my throwing arm has been mixed. My father, I suspect, thought it was kind of cute. He has always operated from the theme that the more ornery I was, the better were my chances for survival. At any rate, he gave me a cast-iron skillet one Christmas with the explanation, "Here, sweet. Here's one you won't be able to break." I have a Deep South

friend with some dish-demolishing experience of her own
who expresses reasonable logic, "Bettah bre-ak a dish
than bre-ak a ha-id!" My mother and children think a parent
should act like a parent.

David has never paid too much attention to these emotional
demonstrations. His tolerance of me through the years
has been exceptional. I do think it's interesting to note,
however, that the jar of junior baby food was the last thing I
ever pitched. Maybe this is because it was also the first
time David, my husband, sat me down, dared to endure my
scathing glances, and asked, "Why are you so angry?"

We sat in the living room, my husband and I, while the light
from the March dusk filtered through the rooms with a
softness, making the toys and havoc and my reaction seem,
if not absurd, at least a little silly.

As I calmed down, I gave an explanation that seemed to
me to be obvious. I was angry because the house was in a
mess, and I would have to clean it again. I was always
cleaning and everyone was always messing. It seemed as
though I spent my entire life picking up after people. I would
never be able to do the things I really wanted to do!

"What is it you really want to do?" he continued, probing.

On the surface that query does not seem to bear much
weight. In actuality, it brought me profoundly to terms with
myself. I responded quickly. The answer was on the tip
of my soul. *I wanted to write.*

To write. To write. To write. To spill some of the building
overflow of emotion and thoughts and feelings that dammed
within me. To wind my way through those inner labyrinths
and find the exits, then tell about my journey on paper. To
observe joy—the pain and delight of it—then express it.
To impregnate a word with meaning, then give it birth. To
mold phrases, manipulate rhythms—to give them flesh.
To breathe print into life—then plant it in the soul of another.
I knew what I really wanted to do.

He was quiet for a while, then asked, "What is stopping
you? What can I do that will help you? Are the children and I
keeping you from writing? Are you angry with us?"

Why is it some awakenings are slow buddings—like

unexpected flowers unfolding? And why is it that some come tumbling like avalanches which almost destroy us with their impact?

This awful moment of truth was the tumbling kind—it was not husband or offspring or house that were stopping me. They were only the excuses beneath which I hid. *It was I— I myself, that was keeping me from writing.*

It was my sin, my very own, the sin which always popped to mind when preachers pointed fingers—procrastination. It was again the lack of discipline which had haunted me since childhood, my fatal flaw of putting things off. Though I had taken myself to task during my fourth pregnancy, and though I had established order, finally, in the household, I had not as yet benefited from all that effort! I had been frittering away the months since that child was born.

I was my own worst enemy, my own greatest deterrent. It was myself with whom I was deeply, inexorably at war. In bare, bald self-confrontation, I realized *I was angry with me!*

Moments of truth come rarely, and when they do, they are precious. One had best heed their intimate revelations. I dragged the typewriter out onto the dining room table and set up my office in the center of the house. I learned to write with toddlers crawling at my feet; I developed the capacity to hold an idea while I attended to a crisis or paused to stick dinner in the oven. I kept the writing going in my mind while I picked up toys and soothed siblings, and then rushed back to get it out on paper before the concepts were gone. I developed the capacity to concentrate in the midst of any kind of confusion. I learned to write at night when the house was quiet, and to write in the afternoon when the infants were napping, even though I have always realized that mornings were the best time for my creative efforts. There were to be no excuses!

Finally, with the initial flush of early successes upon me, I set apart a small closet in the master bedroom, 4½' by 3½', for my writing nook, found an interested editor, began sending out free-lance material, hired a housekeeper to come in three afternoons a week, and hoped to God I would make enough money to pay her.

FIFTEEN
THE BOX

" . . . Karen, well, she's like any other, average businessman's wife."

A neighbor had just introduced us to the couple who had most recently moved to our gregarious block. David had been tagged as the "resident preacher who stays up all Saturday night to get his Sunday sermon ready and who isn't interested in boozing—but a nice guy anyway." But I, I was "like any other, average businessman's wife."

The remark haunted me for days. I think it was meant as a compliment, and I even laughed about it, *but in my heart I knew it was true*. My brand of Christianity didn't make me essentially different from these moral, community-minded, family-centered friends, many of whom admittedly didn't believe in God.

I still had a superficial faith, an average Christianity. I wasn't really significantly different from any other believer's wife. My home, my clothes, my learning, my entertainment—all came before my God. The externals were in order. We went regularly to church. I gave verbal witness to my religiosity—but the internal, hidden depths of my soul were not in inexorable union with my Creator. I knew it—and so did they, my neighbors.

My social assimilation had gone too far. I was trying hard to be one of their kind. I had succeeded. I had traded in the party dress worn in my father's house, for street clothes, and now it was time to search for robes of a different order altogether.

There is an old allegory about the man who has lived all his life in a cave and about his eventual response to light when brought into the glimmering, shining outside. An allegory of my life might better be represented by a dark room-like box with boarded windows and barred door. As long as I am content living in the blackness of this limited dimension, I function fairly well. At least the interior is secure, it is well known. It is familiar and without surprises.

However, through the rough-sawn wood which boards the windows, there enters a shaft of light. This is none of my doing; the ray is from the outside of my little world. It exists apart from me. My responses to it in the past have been several: "How nice. A small light is shining. Isn't that interesting." Or "I wish it would go away. It disturbs my sleep."

Fortunately, I have developed another reaction to the light lately. It is one of wonder. "Why is it here? And where does it come from? Is there more of it? And if so, how can more of it be obtained?"

A meager ray struggles through the boarded windows of my dark world. I do not really know it is dark, since this is all I have experienced—except now, now there is a small glimmer of contrast. What will happen if the shutters are torn from the frame? Will there be more light?

Without tools (and I have none), I approach the crack through which the gleam flutters. With bare hands, I begin to shake the boards a little. Aha! A piece is loose here. I knock it out of the way. A positive glare (or what seems like a glare to me, it is really quite dim) floods through the place where the discarded sliver had been. It flashlights itself into a corner of my home. Hm-m-m-m, this place is not so comfortable as it seemed. It is rather filthy. I gather the dirt revealed into a pile and then painstakingly throw the refuse out the tiny hole I have made through my own efforts.

In the spare haze caused by this phenomenon, I can see that there are other windows in my room, each tightly nailed shut. I begin to investigate each, to find a chink here, another

ill-fitting place there. I wonder if the light will come in
from them too, or if it shines only on that side. Ah, here is a
loose nail. I pull it out, wriggle it, really. As I press hard against
the loosened section of board, it breaks, then falls. Ah, yes!
Illumination pours in through this little spot. It falls to the
opposite corner of the floor. There *is* light on this side of my
little home!

Again, I find rubble in the spotlit corner. I had not been
aware of it being there. With much effort I gather it to discard,
but some pieces are too large to press through my tiny
holes. I will have to enlarge them to get rid of this stuff. I push
and pull and break some more. I shove the junk against the
holes and out it goes. That's much better. There's more
space in here now; no wonder I kept bumping into myself in
the dark. How beautiful the light is! Sometimes it is rosy,
sometimes it is pure white. How did I ever live without it?

One day I get another idea. If I could get the boards off all
the windows on one side, wouldn't this whole room be
flooded with glory? It seems like a rather fine conception.
A large task, to be sure—I have no crowbars or hammers—
but a worthy occupation. To live in light—that sounds sensible
enough.

So the work begins, and like all major remodelings, it is an
agonizing undertaking, more arduous than I had ever
imagined. My fingernails are torn to the quick from clawing
at this relentless wood, my knuckles are skinned and
scraped, but the windows on one wall are finally freed! The
light falls in radiant shafts. It warms me, and suddenly
I realize in what utter poverty and neglect I have been living.

Not only does the light pour in, but I can see out through
the bars that still remain. It is beautiful out there! What does it
look like on the other sides of the room? What are these
hills and waters I see? What are the things I smell, the fresh
odors which flood my poor domicile with their delights? What
will I discover if I tear the boards from the windows on the
other walls?

So the task is begun, a little frantically. I am anxious to
know what I have been missing by living in this narrow,
limited hole. My hands are bloodied, their flesh torn. I have
lunged with my shoulders, raising bruises and welts; I

have kicked with my feet. Even my teeth have been taken against the barricades that would raise the slightest barrier between me and this translucence.

At last! Each of the windows is unboarded. I fling them open with a cry. How beautiful it is! How utterly beyond my imagining! How precious! The brilliance pours in and the vistas around me are breathtaking. All the garbage I have lived with, without knowing it, is discarded, the room is cleared.

I rest from my efforts, for they have exhausted me. But wait ... wait... what is that out there? *Someone is walking among the trees, on that good green. Someone is out there, freed from the dark cabins. Someone is enjoying his liberty!*

A force surges through me. I do not want to live the rest of my life in this box! I want out! I want out! I want to walk on the clean lawn too. I don't want to bang forever against these four walls! I don't think I like it here anymore! I want out! I want out!

So it is with spiritual awakening. The light shines into our darkened world, into the places we have always lived, where we are comfortable because we have known no other. It illumines us. By coincidence, seeming chance, it turns our heads. We notice it and want more. We claw at the boarded windows. We clean away the filth. The shutters are torn off, the light floods us.

Now to others, it may seem as though our accomplishments are rather profound. That is reasonable since many of them are still living in the blackness. However, those of us who have looked out of those windows have seen something more. We have smelled it. Others walk there, why not we? We want out!

I knew that for me it was time. The moment had come to seek and find that supernatural Christianity, the kind that exists outside of the dark boxes of our lives; to discover the secret of that New Testament power which transforms, to search for the formula of new creation.

The awakenings had done their work in me. From the first small shaft of light which had tumbled me, yawning and stretching, from my dreams, I was now living in a room full of light. Opening my eyes to this daylight had taken years.

It was time now to become unlike the average woman, everyman's wife, to hear that distant call, like some familiar horn blowing from the wispy memories of childhood. The moment had come to answer my own, my very special summons.

II SUMMONS

He will not refuse one who is so blithe to go to him.

—Sir Thomas More
A Man for All Seasons by Robert Bolt

ONE
A WOMAN OF GOD

Here is a woman who can "Titus" you!

We had been attending a Bible conference, another family vacation during which David had been invited to minister. I was seated at the head table during the women's luncheon, listening to the featured address given by a veteran missionary with an incredible tale to tell.

Captured during the Second World War on the island of Celebes in the South China Seas, she had spent the next six years in a Japanese forced labor camp with fifteen hundred women and children. When she was released at the end of the war, she was only twenty-six years of age. She weighed less than ninety pounds, her hair had turned prematurely gray, and she had multiple nutritional deficiencies.

She had lost her husband, who died in a men's camp, after suffering from exposure, starvation, and mistreatment. Yet through all her losses she had experienced God's miraculous intervention and care for her life.

"They who know their God shall do exploits..." she quoted, and she revealed incident after incident when, in the darkest of circumstances, God had quietly but definitely revealed his Presence.

I was moved beyond my understanding.

Certainly, I thought, this is a woman of faith who can help me become the person of God I was created to be.

In the remaining day and a half of the conference I had no opportunity to engage her in conversation, and I was much too shy to seek her out or to impose myself into her life at the breakfast table the next morning.

"Oh, David," I sighed as we started our eight-hour drive home, the car now loaded with four happy children, each content with the family vacation. "I wish you could have heard her speak..." Then I proceeded to relate as much as I remembered of her remarkable tale, while the miles flowed past and unaccountable tears streamed down my cheeks.

Arriving home, we found the vacation was soon diminished as we resumed our urgent daily responsibilities. But I kept mulling over and over those tales of God intervening in our century, even though the events had occurred some thirty years before.

I had been impressed with this missionary's knowledge of the Word—it had seemed so organic in her life, so much a part of her experience. To her the Scriptures were a living thing, applicable to each bright or terrible moment. I began to read my Bible regularly, to attempt to establish some kind of firm schedule of study. I pored over Hebrews and discovered that I did not comprehend. I agonized over John 15, Christ's exposition on the vine and the branches; I reread it four or five times at one sitting and realized that this too was beyond my insight. At this point I heard that small but firm voice whispering, *Karen Mains, you know more than you have experienced.*

It was true. I knew it was true. I had a knowledge about God which far surpassed my experience of him. My acquaintance with him was negligible. Yet, even my knowledge was fractured, incomplete. Somehow the theoretical and the experiential needed to be wedded in my life, so that each reinforced the other, and both could develop hand in hand.

Usually it takes me a while to effect any new venture. My beginnings are halting and painfully slow. Once underway, however, they seem to attain rapid momentum. These rapid implementations often leave me out of breath.

I realized that I read everything, from best-sellers to news magazines to the classics, but I rarely read the Word of God. How could I possibly know about God or know him by acquaintance, if I never spent any time reading his written revelation? Tearfully, I confessed my neglect to our congregation and vowed that I would not read anything but the Bible until I had "seen his glory"! And I didn't. It was a year and a half before I picked up any other reading material. By that time I could say that I knew more about God and that I had also met him in my experience.

One day soon after this, our phone rang and I was pleased to hear the voice of the wife of the chaplain of a nearby Christian college. "Karen," she said. "Mrs. _____ will be in the area for several weeks. Do you know of any churches that might be able to use her in one of their services?"

She was referring to the very woman who had so moved me at the summer missionary conference. I certainly did know of *one* church that would be delighted to have her speak.

To give credit where credit is due, the greatest consistent spiritual influence in my life has undoubtedly been my husband. However, there have been shadowed moments of soul crises when I have been unalterably influer 'ed by certain Christian women. Though there have not been many, each has been mighty in faith. Some have spoken to me from the sketchy chronicles of history, others have intersected my meanderings by strategic divine purpose. The result for me has always been deep spiritual regenesis.

"I don't understand why that talk made such a difference in your life," puzzled a friend, after she listened to a cassette recording of this woman speaking. The answer is simply that God calls each of us uniquely at certain moments. If we are ready to hear his voice, we can be radicalized while others are only temporarily interrupted. At this precise moment, he is not calling our friend's name. He is breathing our own. While we are gripped in a petit mal of sudden personal significance, others may notice only slight alterations in our behavior. But we understand that permanent personality changes are being forged.

I was simply hungry for someone who had experienced as much of God as she knew of him. I had a deep need for an unordinary woman of faith with whom I could rub shoulders. I am convinced, in looking back, that it had to be a feminine model.

If Christian women have a common flaw, it is that we continually settle for being less than what God intends us to be. We desperately need examples of women who *were* not and *are* not content to be less than spiritually significant. How rarely does the modern woman bend her being in the awful conflict with the Angelic Wrestler. We are afraid to grip his garments as Jacob did, until, with our nails torn, clothes disarrayed, hip crippled, we gasp—"Bless me! I will not let you go until you have blessed me!" I suppose we don't encounter him in this way because we have allowed ourselves to become spiritually passive. We think this kind of desire is unwomanly.

Where are the women who will be examples of those who weep, "O God! What is it you want me to be? Name who I am before your face. I will not let you go until you have touched me, until you have molded the new creation of yourself in my flesh." Sadly, those who are willing to be crippled by him in order to receive his blessing are few.

Yet we have predecessors, women who were giants of faith. The Shunamite woman laid her lifeless son on a cot and hurried to the prophet Elisha. Seeing her coming from afar he sent his messenger to ask, "Is it well with you? Is it well with your husband? Is it well with your child?" The vision of that dead body must have been beating in her brain, yet she called out, a cry for all time, "It is well."

Mary sat at the feet of Jesus, listening to his teachings, a woman among men, not debating or disputing, but pondering in the quiet of her contemplative heart. Like the disciples, she heard his words concerning imminent death, but unlike them it was she who sensed his coming Gethsemane, who intuitively felt the grief building in his soul. She responded by pouring costly perfume over those same feet she had washed so often after a day's dusty journey, and which she was to see crushed beneath the pounded spike.

It was a girl faced with the awesome overcoming of the Holy Spirit who whispered, "Behold, I am the handmaid of the Lord; let it be unto me according to your word." It was the courage of women who breathed broken love beneath the cross, who did not desert Jesus in his agony. It was women who dared the disfavor of godless temple soldiers guarding a tomb.

Oh, that I might cry, *All is well*, when faced with the overwhelming sorrows of life. All is well in his Presence, all is well. Oh, that I might sit at his feet to learn the deep mysteries of faith, that I might hear the things others are too busy to heed, that I might pour myself out in worship and service despite the shattering circumstances of unknown tomorrows. Lord, help me to maintain vigil in the face of death, to share this world's agony. Make me brave beside tombs and create in me a heart that always wants to say, "Behold your handmaiden. Let it be unto me according to your word."

Countless others are our predecessors. True, unlike their male counterparts, their histories are sparse and fragmented. The dramas of some will never be revealed until eternity reigns over time. I attended a lecture by Roland Bainton, considered to be one of the foremost authorities on the Reformation, who mentioned that women were integral to that period of spiritual renewal. There exists adequate testimony that women too "suffered mocking and scourging, and even chains and imprisonment. They were stoned, they were sawn in two, they were killed with the sword; they went about in skins of sheep and goats, destitute, afflicted, ill-treated—of whom the world was not worthy—wandering over deserts and mountains, and in dens and caves of the earth."

All of these, our foremothers, had experienced unalterable spiritual renaissance. In one way or another they brought God's redemption to the societies which surrounded them. In the little time they had, with meager means, lives shortened by childbearing, faced with daily disaster, often uneducated, they significantly influenced their world with a living belief in a God who was there.

Now, here was one coming to my own home, a woman who knew God—knew him by acquaintance as well as knew about him.

I was shameless. I grilled her. I robbed her of her sleep with my inquisition. I sat at the foot of her bed and asked for more. I was hungry for reality, to be regaled with stories of God's power, to be fed with the mighty accounts of his acts in my generation. Through some unaccountable mystery of God's grace, she spent three weekends in our home.

I absorbed everything she had to give to me that smacked of
spiritual maturity.

Give to me she did, two remarkable lessons of faith that
winged me on my way to God.

Because I had excellent parents, I grew up with a
well-developed sense of God as my Heavenly Father. Their
example had not hindered, but indeed had helped me
grow into a trusting, comfortable relationship with God as
Parent. This one member of the Trinity I felt I comprehended
fairly well.

My concepts of the other members of that Unity, however,
were vastly underdeveloped. Christ, God the Son, was not
much more to me than a Sunday school paper figure, and the
Holy Spirit—well, who or what was he?

This missionary entered my life exactly at the time I was
beginning to grapple with the meaning of the Holy Spirit. I
had read everything put out by the charismatic publishing
houses on the baptism of the Spirit, and certain Scriptures
were used to prove certain presuppositions. Then I read
everything on the Holy Spirit published by the opposing
groups. Totally confused, I conducted a word survey
throughout the entire Bible, using my concordance to record
every reference to the Spirit—and still I had no answer.

Interviewing my new acquaintance, I inquired, "What is
your doctrine of the Holy Spirit?" Surely someone as godly as
she would have a position I could emulate. She shared
her beliefs, without dogmatism, then very wisely gave to me
her first gift: "You know, Karen, the Spirit is able to teach you
everything you need to know." These were the last words
I heard her speak as I dropped her off to catch an airplane at
O'Hare Airport. They stayed with me, stamped indelibly,
black-printer's-pad fashion.

Along with this—the Spirit is able to teach you everything
you need to know—was another phrase that dropped
casually from our whirlwind conversations. "We take so much
time talking to God that we never have any time to listen
to him." I suppose this took on unusual significance for me
because I could see in this woman that quality of always
being in a state of receiving, a quietness of spirit which
demonstrated to me the true import of her verbal expressions.

She had heard the Lord's word coming to her in the blackest of circumstances, at the point of death, with her executioner swinging a sword above her head, during bombings, in overwhelming grief at the word of the death of her husband, in the solitary hole of confinement in the Kempetai (Secret Service) prison, before the anguished cries of natives gone wild with cannibalistic bloodlust. It had preserved her, reassured her, comforted her, and given her calm. Indeed, because of her knowing of him, she had done exploits. I wanted to know him in such a way.

Briefly, she touched my life, but sometimes the brief encounters are all we need. It was enough time for it to do what God intended.

I began to go before him each day and cry, "O Lord, I am just like a little child when it comes to spiritual knowing; what is it you have to teach me today?"

This one theme, played without variation for months, combined with my deliberate poring over the written Word, began to work wonders in my spirit. I believed he could teach me; I had seen someone who had been taught by him. I believed I could hear him speak to me; I had seen someone who had heard him speak. I would open the Scriptures and read, then sit and listen with my notebook and my pencil ready in case anything important dropped into my heart and mind. Sometimes the listening alone would go on for a half an hour.

Simply, he began to alter me. Yes, he was perfectly able to teach me everything I needed to know. I discovered that there is no more apt a teacher. When I stopped talking and started listening, I began to develop the capacity to hear. I have learned that he is always the source of deep spiritual growth.

Dear Teacher,

I have sat in your classroom daily and I know that your pedagogy is unsurpassed. I praise you for your gentle instruction, for the fact that you never expound truth without also drawing fitting applications. I praise you for your professorial discipline. It is loving and wise.

I also want to thank you for those humans who have sat quietly at your feet, learning, and who then have allowed themselves to be windows through whom your light shines.

Yes, I praise you that you are the Ultimate Theologian, and I will be eternally grateful for those special women who have Titused me.

Amen.

TWO
EPIPHANIES

The next few months were the fall of that year—September, October, and November. They were a rapid and breathless succession of epiphanies, episodes of one kind or another in which he revealed himself to me, and the more I saw of him, the more I wanted.

My private litany continued; "Teach me what it is I need to know—"

He showed me that at present my house and the decorating of it were more important to me than him. I spent hours musing about the placement of imaginary pictures—things we didn't even yet possess, wasted precious energy stewing over other material needs, invested afternoons roaming through antique and junk shops hunting for bargains which then required days of my time to repair and restore. It was a matter of choice. Did I want to spend the time getting to know him, or did I want to have the most cleverly eclectic house in the whole church?

My readings in the Gospels at this time were particularly pregnant: "Put ye first the kingdom of God and his righteousness and all these things will be added unto you . . ." I chose. I decided the house would be my mortification. I was embarrassed by it anyway, and felt I might as well use it to kill desire. I recognized that I used shopping as a boost when I felt low. Even window shopping, when I didn't

actually buy anything, gave me a little shot of adrenaline.
I suspected a hunger for material things had become a
substitution for a hunger for God.

At this point I made another vow. The house would stay
exactly as it was. I would accept gratefully everything we had
and everything we didn't have. I promised the Lord I
would not enter a store for a three-month period except for
necessary purchases of food, and then I limited myself to
spending what a mother on welfare would receive for a family
our size.

In essence, I went on a shopping fast. In place of the time
I would normally spend decorating a house, or fantasizing
about decorating a house, or shopping for things to fill that
house, I determined to give those hours to the Lord.

"Teach me what it is you want me to know," I prayed. He
showed me that I was filling my mind with unholy things.
I was allowing the television to inculcate in me the banal, the
carnal, the mediocre. "The eye is the lamp of the body.
So, if your eye is sound, your whole body will be full of light;
but if your eye is not sound, your whole body will be full
of darkness." "Enter by the narrow gate; for the gate is wide and
the way is easy, that leads to destruction, and those who
enter by it are many. For the gate is narrow and the way is
hard, that leads to life, and those who find it are few." Here
was a standard of righteousness I had hitherto neglected.
One of the children dropped our portable TV. We placed
it on the trash pile rather than making any attempt to repair it.

"What is it you have to teach me, Lord?" I discovered
that the object lessons were endless. All of life became a tool
of teaching in his hands.

A close friend was released from a psychiatric ward and
came directly to our house to talk with David. Never having
seen, firsthand, the results of personality disintegration, I was
totally unprepared. This good friend who had been so close
to me, a brother in intellectual pursuits, my encourager
in writing, flew at me verbally in such a way that I ran to my
room, leaving him in David's more capable hands.

Alone I wept, torn in horror, "O God, look at him! He's
nothing but a bundle of bared nerve endings of ego!"

Suddenly, it was as though God held a mirror to that man,

and turned it on my own soul. In it I viewed my own
reflected countenance. *That's the way you all are without your
masks*, I heard.

I looked and it was true. There were all my bared nerve
endings of ego: my practice of entering a room personality-
first, my habit of dominating conversations with me-me-me,
my subtle but arrogant exercises in superiority. He shone
a speculum on me that I could not escape. It was my own
ghastly ego that was keeping me from him.

"If any man would come after me, let him deny himself
and take up his cross and follow me. For whoever would save
his life will lose it, and whoever loses his life for my sake will
find it. For what will it profit a man, if he gains the whole
world and forfeits his life?" Instinctively, I knew I would
have to allow him to crucify those parts of me that prevented
me from experiencing him.

A small rug in our center hall had been given to us by some
close friends. It was made in a German town which has
opened factories to provide useful employment for the
mentally and emotionally ill. It was three paces long, and I
traversed it a hundred times a day. At first I breathed
the three syllables of the name of our friend who had
undergone a breakdown.

Step, step, step—I would pray his name going east toward
the kitchen and then as I returned—step, step, step, I would
intone, "And for me." Finally, I stopped the prayers for
him; my need was just as great. "Do thou for me, Lord,"
I cried. "Do thou for me."

The epiphanies continued, too numerous to mention, too
countless to remember. I only knew that there was scarcely a
corner of my life turned, where I didn't discover the
intimations of God. Here was his fingerprint pressed against
my tattered interpretations of holiness. Here was his
solemark indenting my slovenly spiritual disciplines. Veil
after veil he lifted, curtain after curtain. I followed after each
clue, each thread leading from my labyrinth, each pertinent
revelation.

After I had put all other reading aside, Scripture shone with
clarity. Sleepless nights came and the words I had so glibly
memorized as a young girl rolled over and over me, suddenly

infused with meaning. It was as though I had never read or understood it before; it was being made new in me, all new. With the implementation of the shopping fast, the material holds in my life began to dwindle in importance. This house and the things in it, the temporal, the transitory, were not nearly as close to me as they had been. The spiritual was drawing nearer, the world of the Kingdom that is and that will be.

The fall of that year stretched into winter, and I scarcely noticed the blaze of it or the turning. There was another season coming in my soul that was now consuming my attention. It was the autumn of my own discontent, a tilting axis sending me spinning in pursuit of God. I was watching the winter preparations for crucifixion.

"Teach me what it is you want me to know, Lord," I had dared to cry. He taught me that it was himself I wanted and needed and desired, not my intellectual pursuits, not the cuddling of this good world, not even myself. It was he I wanted and none other. None other would I have.

O God, I have tasted Thy goodness, and it has both satisfied me and made me thirsty for more. I am painfully conscious of my need of further grace. I am ashamed of my lack of desire. O God, the Triune God, I want to want Thee; I long to be filled with longing; I thirst to be made more thirsty still. Show me Thy glory, I pray Thee, that so I may know Thee indeed. Begin in mercy a new work of love within me. Say to my soul, "Rise up, my love, my fair one, and come away." Then give grace to rise and follow Thee up from this misty lowland where I have wandered so long. In Jesus' Name, Amen.

—A. W. Tozer, *The Pursuit of God*

THREE
WHO CALLS?

Who calls? Who calls in this deep night?

Plunging out of sleep, my heart fluttering, I know someone has called my name. Listening in this darkened room, in this quiet house, I hear the soft slumber-breath of children nearby, notice the whisk of cars brushing fallen leaves off the street.

What voice cried in this empty night, gently, urgently, "Karen!"

Was it some remnant memory of days gone past, some soundwave capturing me as I hovered on the sleepy edge of consciousness?

Was it my father's voice? No—he always restores my name to its Swedish form, "*Kah*ren! *Kah*ren Sue!"

Had someone really called my name? The bedside clock read 2:00.

Settling back onto the pillows and giving my startled heart a chance to regulate itself, I remembered this happening to me in childhood, a voice calling me from sleep. I liked to pretend it was God and that I was the child Samuel. "Here am I," I would whisper. "Here am I."

For months I had been seeking the God of Samuel, that God who interjects his presence into human affairs. Weary of ordinary, carbon-copy Christianity, I had been hunting the

supernatural. Like that of the psalmist David, mine was
a soulish ardor:

As a hart longs
  for flowing streams,
so longs my soul
  for thee, O God.
My soul thirsts for God,
  for the living God.
When shall I come and behold
  the face of God?

                                                      Psalm 42:1, 2

I had become a thirsty vagabond sniffing the air for the barest
hints of moisture, a starveling whose innards melted at
the faintest yeasty aroma of bread.

"When shall I come and behold the face of God?" Surely
around the next bend, at some surprising turning, I would
catch a glimpse, see a shadow of his form. I was footsore from
this following after, and the way behind me was littered
with abandoned cargoes, luggage too heavy to carry in my
breathless haste.

Falling asleep that night, I had whispered, "God, I am
panting after you. You have not sated my desire but increased
it. If I don't taste something of yourself soon, a part of
me will be destroyed because of its great need!"

Who calls? I knew now who had breathed, *Karen! Karen!*
and who it was uttering this call. Hurriedly, I grabbed my Bible
and made my way barefoot downstairs to my husband's
study. "O God," I whispered. "My very marrow is famished
for you. Hasn't the moment come to feed me with yourself?"

There are times when it is quiet and when we are spiritually
sensitive and his Spirit is able to commune with our spirit.
This was one of those intervals. In the silence I heard him
say, *Read 1 John*.

As a teenager I had memorized the three epistles of John,
and I was well aware of the contents of this letter. It dealt with
walking in fellowship with God and with loving our Christian
brethren.

"But, Lord," I protested. "You know I love the people

in our church. I have exceptional abilities at loving. I may even love people too much."

The inward, quiet nudging came again: *Confess to me the names of all those you don't love.*

Appalled, I discovered there were twenty-seven names! Humiliated, I confessed each one.

Oh, the mysterious mirror of God! For months I had been searching for him only to be confounded with a glimpse into that glass held by his hand. He forced me to look and therein discover my true visage. Self, this ugly, gloating, prideful self, was all I saw. Self without its masks, without its petty pretenses, was what continually kept me from him and constantly fogged my vision of the elusive spiritual.

My self-righteousness came back to me—"I may even love people too much." Chagrined, I sank to my knees, my soul choked with embarrassment. "Forgive, Lord. Forgive this pride, this charlatan ego. Give me your love and teach me what it means to love."

The Word again: *Now. Now you may read Romans 12:1.* Trembling, I opened my Bible to that familiar passage, "Present your bodies as a living sacrifice, holy and acceptable to God, which is your spiritual worship."

The time indeed had come. Reaching up, I flicked off the study lamp and then, in heightened agony of soul, cast myself on my face on the floor. Many before me have thrown themselves prone, have discarded sandals and shoes, have discovered tongues cleaving to mouthtops, all because they have suddenly encountered the Living Presence. I prostrated myself, and by this common act plunged into the unknown, my spirit yet shouting unutterably, "I give you all I am! Now you give me all you have for me!"

How do we describe sacred moments? The ancients talked of burning bushes and fire on the mountains, whirlwinds followed by still, small voices, the glory of God filling temples —yet even the tongues of sages and poets are inadequate. All I know was that an immense quiet yawned before me. I was utterly afraid, consumed with a holy awe because I knew, knew with the spiritual senses, that I was being possessed, being overcome with the awful Presence of the Almighty.

Terror struck me. I suddenly doubted. "How do you know

you are being possessed by supernatural good and not supernatural evil?"

Doggedly, I answered back. "I asked for him. It is he whom I have invited. It is he who is calling me. It is he who will come." The doubts fled.

"Possess me then," I cried. "Possess me totally. Don't leave a part of me the same. Touch the inner depth and the outer surfaces. Fill my mind, my hands, my soul. And if you want (I had been afraid of this)—Lord, touch my tongue."

My child, the Possessor replied. *Out of the abundance of the heart the mouth speaks.*

"Then the heart, my Lord." I could barely whisper it. "Touch this beating, wayward, harlot heart."

How long I lay prone, I don't know. Time is human. God is always above and beyond it. Consequently, he does what he wills with our moments. Eventually, the fear subsided. Eternity seemed to have withdrawn. I sat up and drew my knees to my chin.

This had not been an emotional experience. I had not wept or shouted. It had not been ecstatic. I had not spoken in tongues or been filled with heavenly laughter. Yet there was a quiet joy, a calm, bright joy, and I began to sing a silly little ditty, the melody and lyric of which I had never heard before. There seemed to be only one word which sounded like: "Henani." So I sang that word over and over, happily, like a young child with an interesting sound, "He-nani-nani. He-nani-nani. He-nani-nani, nani-nani, ni."

After a short while I began to wonder—what will happen several months from now? I knew I was not a giant of faith. I was a very ordinary woman. Perhaps I would begin to doubt this moment. As a child of my times, maybe I would convince myself that I had simply participated in some psychological farce.

"Lord," I prayed, "I don't know if this is allowed, but I am afraid of the days to come. Would it be too much to ask you to mark me in some way, to give me a sign to hang onto so I will be firmly convinced this has been of you?"

Instantly, my hands were filled with rushing life. Something surged through them, a luminescence that startled me. Nothing in my past experience, my religious background had prepared me for this. The fundamentalists were my fathers, the evangelicals my guardians. All I could think of were Jesus' words when he was touched in the jostling crowd by the woman with an issue of blood. He perceived that power had gone out of him. This sensation was beyond my experience; it was also beyond my knowing, but a sign it was, indeed, a surety I had not anticipated when I made my request.

What does one do with hands shimmering with life-force? One of the children cried out in his sleep. Leaving the little room which had served so well as my altar, I climbed the stairs and made my way to the bed of each sleeping child. Carefully, lest this strange energy should wake them, I placed my hands on each little head, blessing them all in the name of the Lord, setting them aside for future ministry, calling out God's gifts in them, pouring this confusing spiritual unknown into their slumbering bodies.

Then I crawled back into the place from which I had heard a voice calling my name while I slept. I little knew then what he holds in store for those who hear and answer his call. That was just as well. I too returned to dreams, but they were filled with wonder and with echoes of the Magnificat rolling over and over to some hidden, universal rhythm.

My soul-doth mag-nify-the Lord/ and my-spirit-rejoices in-God my-Savior,/ for he-has regarded-the low-estate-of his-handmaiden/ his handmaiden/ his handmaiden/ his handmaiden . . .

FOUR
THE EXCHANGED LIFE

How comforting it is to realize that the unusual spiritual experience for which we have no name is not so unusual after all.

I was greatly soothed by V. Raymond Edman's little book *They Found the Secret*, in which he chronicles the spiritual crises of twenty-one different lives. During my search for the Holy Spirit, before I began my reading fast, I had picked up this volume, hoping to discover a "how-to-do-it manual." Instead, I realized from it that the Lord's work is as diverse in the lives of his children as their faces are from each other. J. Hudson Taylor, John Bunyan, Amy Carmichael, Charles G. Finney—each one had been radically altered at some time in his spiritual growth, but no one story was a duplicate of the other.

This is the beauty and majesty of God. He calls each of us and draws each of us and molds each of us in his own way, suited to our particular personalities and needs.

However, as Dr. Edman points out, though the details of God's work are different in each life, there is a pattern for deeper spiritual growth that seems to be quite common. I was tremendously soothed when, months after having been called from my bed by the Lord, I picked up this volume once again and found that his delineation fitted my experience like a glove.

First of all, Dr. Edman maintains, there is an *awareness of need* which occurs as a basic step at the beginning of each of our journeys into the spiritual. For me, this came in a series of awakenings scattered over a period of years. There was the city, having children and being responsible for their upbringing, and the difficult and delightful ministry of pastoring in a ghetto as well as a cosmopolitan area. There was the fractious rebellion of the generation of the sixties, the struggle to achieve wholeness and personhood, and bombardment by divergent cultural influences—all these were means by which I was brought to terms with the fact that I was needy.

We had been working with many broken people who came to our church, the castoffs of society, those whose creativity had short-circuited them and who were suspect in their own churches. Many of those disenfranchised young adults who were distressed with the dormancy of their churches' social concerns were now suffering from the effects of their indiscriminate protests. I came to the realization that human love was not enough. *I* was not enough to meet the overwhelming dislocation of the lives that surrounded us.

Finally, I became tired of my everywoman's existence and began to long for a Christianity that was filled with the unordinary. What was the power of this new life which I saw so openly proclaimed on every page of my New Testament, and how did one procure it?

Out of this awareness of need, Dr. Edman points out, grows the development of the next step, *an agony of soul*. No more appropriate phrase could be used to describe the awful stirrings which began to consume the internal me. I became hungry for God. All men hunger, but the tragedy of our humanity is that we substitute material realities for the only One who is able to fill our need. "Do not labor for the food which perishes," taught Christ. "But for the food which endures to eternal life. I am the bread of life; he who comes to me shall not hunger, and he who believes in me shall never thirst."

I had become so consumed with a desire for God, for the reality of the spiritual, that I was finally ready to cast aside anything that might seek to fill the cavity that yawned within me, anything that would block me from him.

A friend told me recently, "The bottom line to any contract dealing with spiritual growth is, 'Is there a hunger for God?' " Many of us interpret this to be a kind of passive openness. That is hardly enough. Passivity soon becomes dormancy. No, there must be a deliberate hunt for him which we set into motion, a commitment of purpose from which we will not rest until we have seen its fulfillment. It must indeed be an agony of the soul, one through which we pass, willing to yield all in order to finally cling to our ultimate desire. The psalmist cries, "Thou hast said, 'Seek ye my face.' My heart says to thee, 'Thy face, Lord, do I seek.' Hide not thy face from me."

It is comforting to note that this kind of hunger holds a promise of fulfillment. Christ spoke about this topic in the Beatitudes: "Blessed are they which do hunger and thirst after righteousness; *for they shall be filled.*"

The next step in this classic pattern is wholehearted, *unreserved abandonment* to the Savior. The many different strands of Christianity have chosen various words to describe this act. Hannah Whitall Smith in her much-read *The Christian's Secret of a Happy Life* refers to this as consecration. The Keswick movement might term this the life hid in Christ. Full surrender, yielding, laying one's all on the altar, the exchanged life—all are verbal symbols which are employed to describe this moment of awesome soul release.

The exact details of how a person experiences this release are unique; we must not fall into the trap of attempting to replicate each other's moments of abandon. I may have faced God in an awesome encounter, but others close to me who have yielded inch by inch over the years of their lives, with utter regularity, are as filled with God as I, and many are more so. The point is that eventually, either through long-term process or in one arrested instant, we give to him all that we have. The results are the same, no matter the procedure—lives totally offered in living sacrifice.

Next, there must be an *appropriation* of God's work. God's work in response to man's seeking and abandonment also has many names: baptism of the Spirit, filling of the Spirit, a glory experience, a second grace. Whatever we call it, whether it is accompanied by emotion or ecstasy or by nothing that seems out of the ordinary, we must, because of our mortality, trust that the supernatural has indeed touched our lives at our request and that we will never again be the same. "How do you know you are being possessed by supernatural good and not supernatural evil?" "I asked for God," I cried. "It is he whom I have invited. It is he who is calling me. It is he who will come."

God in his graciousness often gives us objective symbols by which to remember his subjective work. We are so finite, so fragile in our hold on the spiritual. "Raise here a monument," he told the children of Israel countless times. These were memory markers to the miraculous. Our appropriation (oh, we of little faith!) often hangs on these graces—the gift of tongues for some, the breaking of another's well-checked emotions, the remembrance of an interlude we felt was other-worldly, a psychological catharsis—but appropriation we claim. We know that God has touched our lives. We cannot prove it logically. We cannot convince the skeptic. We can only give testimony to our belief that he performed an investiture of himself on our lives.

The last common element in the pattern of deep spiritual growth is that of *abiding*, the very concept that was so confusing to me when I read of it in John 15. The next few years I was to learn well the meaning of vines and branches, of being pruned continuously, of staying close to the side of the Gardener.

Part of learning to abide, for me, meant coming to a knowledge of acquaintance with Christ. I had a well developed sense of God, the Parent. I had been radically filled by the Holy Spirit with whom I soon became intimate, but it was the Son of this Holy Three I needed to learn to welcome fully.

My studies on the Holy Spirit had grounded me. I knew Scripture taught that one of his roles was to teach us of Christ. The cry of the Apostle Paul also became my own, "That I might know him, and the power of his resurrection and the fellowship of his sufferings." This was to come to fruition in the days ahead.

How comforting it was to find that I was surrounded by so

great a cloud of witnesses. I was not some aberrant freak wanting more than it was humanly possible to have.

"I came to love you late," cried Augustine. "I think I have always loved you," cried I, finding my place awkwardly, like a toddler clambering into a seat much too high for him. "I have always loved you," I cry again, my voice cracking slightly, feeling aghast by such imposing companions, one little housewife amongst the godly. "But I have never loved you well, not well at all, not half so much as you have deserved, and not an iota of what I am capable of loving."

Yes, I am a part of this great company. Here are my prototypes. I am not an ugly mutant, a sideshow curiosity. Here they are, foremothers and forefathers, all with testimony of the experience of God. "I know whom I have believed," pledges Job. "I believe whom I have known," challenges John.

"So do I," I whisper from my own timorous throat. "Not well, but I will know him better."

FIVE
THE AWFUL SPLENDOR

I remember him wooing the child I used to be!

There are memories of numerous incidents replete with what I now call "awful splendor." One moment filled with beauty could capture my attention fully, arrest me completely. The quickly inhaled breath, a sense of wonder, my soul expanding with awe; then the aching terror of becoming too much a part of something incomprehensible.

I suppose every artist or musician or poet knows what I mean by the "awful splendor"; yet, I suspect this moment of combined pain and ecstasy is a natural creature-response that the conscious mind often learns to shut out. Perhaps once the lowliest slug admired the rose which now it only chews!

Sunlight transformed black bugs, scrambling through cracks, into glittering scarabs, and left me awed. The common things—rows and rows of captured color, jellies and jams in canning jars; creamy milk in a blue and white china pitcher; the grains of old wood—all these sombered me, worked in me moody meditations. Light, its varied rubies of hue moving from floor to table to walls; light! any form of it, was cause for exultation. Birdsong in the morning; bins of vegetables glowing resplendent in the neighborhood peddler's van; the blazing torch of fall aflame on the pyre of earth—all were unbearable delights.

The days were punctuated by my parents' exclamations,

"Oh, look! Isn't it beautiful!" My father's love for the land, my mother's poetry, all served to heighten my appreciation for the natural world.

The feelings these awful splendors evoked are as real now, incredibly, as though they happened only today. The enchantment of one summer evening is etched on my life like a Gaelic fantasy scene on a glass plate. Small friends and I danced hand in hand on the grassy sward of our city boulevard. Round and round we flew, secure in the tepid moonlight. Laughter and streetlamps and warm darkness, children dancing and hoary dandelion puffs like fluffy earth-stars—all these memories come tumbling, even now, to evoke praise.

Then, however, the moments aroused feelings too deep for a child to share or to identify. Restlessness descended; I would begin to wander like a desert nomad searching for I-knew-not-what, looking for something to do, some oasis of rest uncharted. Drawers were opened and closed, closets explored, books leafed and unread. Was there some way to express the emotions stirred by these maverick prongs? something to make? some reservoir in which to store this overflow?

Too magnificent for a small soul, these reckonings often flooded me, and as a teen I had tearfully concluded that I was a hopeless sentimental, a slave of my emotions. Fat toddlers playing in the dirt of neighbors' yards, light slanting at unexpected angles, the variegated greens of spring, all could produce that ache in my inner self. My days turned on the moods of the moments.

One day I took the Webster's down from its shelf. My finger ran down the pages:

sen-ti-men-tal   1. Of the nature of, or characterized or dominated by, sentiment; as sentimental motives. 2. Having an excess of sentiment or having an excess of sensibility; affectedly tender; mawkishly emotional.

In cold print, the definition seemed unduly harsh. "*Mawkishly emotional*"! I knew I would have to guard against these willful prongs, lest they dominate me, reduce me to tears at vulnerable moments, humiliate me with their mawkishness. Early, I gave my head authority over my heart.

Nathaniel Hawthorne's *The Scarlet Letter* influenced me at this point while I was in high school. An astute English teacher underlined a prevailing theme in that classic religious allegory. "Hawthorne," she observed, "believed that intellect should dominate emotion. If the pattern is reversed, the results will always be regrettable."

It seems I implemented that principle well. "We never worried about you when you were dating," my mother recently confided to me. "Daddy always said, 'Don't worry about Karen. Her head rules her heart.' "

No matter how much I kept a handle on the emotive part of me, I nevertheless was aware that something about me was different from other people. This conclusion was based not only on personal suspicions, but on the comments of others. Once while riding with a carload of girl friends, I remember making a comment about some now forgotten topic of conversation. The mother who was driving actually braked the car to a halt, pulled over to the side of the road, turned around to look at me, and demanded, "Karen Burton, how old *are* you?"

While I was still stumbling to keep from tripping over my own feet, I found that people had put me on pedestals. "Don't your ideas ever turn off?" was a comment I heard frequently, often tinged with awe. "You're the most creative person I know," was another. In my adult years, a close friend summarized what I had finally come to accept, "You're weird, Karen Mains. You're as weird as I am. You may look like you have it all together on the outside, but on the inside you're as weird as can be!"

All of us, I suppose, feel a certain sense of alienation from our fellow human beings, but for the creative person, it is often a fearful given. A research project which studied highly creative children reported that they were "often estranged," that many of them had a feeling of "being destined," that they "preferred to work, in fact enjoyed working alone."

The artist soon discovers the world is not visually the same for him as it is for other people, the musician is caught up in an interior vault of melody and harmony and sound. He hears things other people don't hear. As a child, I observed my father's colleagues, all musical virtuosos. There was no doubt about it, they were different. Some of them were downright strange. They had the same flaws as other people, only theirs seemed enlarged, grander than life.

In my early perusals of literature, the fact was soon readily apparent that most great writers were also a little strange. They either died early deaths, burned out because art had consumed them, or manifested odd psychological symptoms. The literary imagination seemed to exact costly tolls. Dostoevsky, Honoré de Balzac, Edgar Allen Poe, Kafka—these were just a few of the many listed on the high mortality rolls, those whose genius seemed to be sacrificed to their work.

An interesting quote from *The Literary Imagination, Psychoanalysis and the Genius of the Writer*, says: "In the *Medical Record*, June 15, 1912, there occurs the statement that 'apparently no writer can dare to aspire to literary distinction without running the risk of submitting to psychological dissection. . . . In many instances it is no longer a question as to whether a certain genius was insane or not. The modern query is, From what form of insanity did he suffer?' "

The life and deterioration of Van Gogh—whose paintings are my favorite among the impressionists, his work is so filled with godly exuberance—impressed me. Yet even I who loved his art could identify the insane exclamations in his brushstrokes. Hemingway's suicide in 1961 set off quiet reverberations in me: "See, this is the end of those who dare to live by the pen." I was eighteen at the time and my contemporaries were graduating from high school, commencing all the activities inherent to that age. I was getting married and mourning Hemingway. His death was another ruler by which I measured the destructive quality of the creative nature.

Here I was with these wild, errant stabs of joy and terror that seemed to descend from without. Of their own initiative they appeared, frightening in their capacity to overwhelm me. As many appearances of normalcy as possible were maintained. I never told anyone that I had read Shakespeare's

Complete Works at the age of ten! (I didn't *understand* what I was reading, I just loved it.) No small soul ever guarded the sentient any more than I. My cognitive side was given absolute control lest I eventually be mastered, be undone.

After my fearful but determined abandonment to the Holy Spirit, a beautiful thing began to occur in me. I put into his hands my all, which included both the cognitive and the emotive. He began to teach me that he was perfectly able to guard this frightening area of my complicated being. It was no longer my responsibility to pace in endless guard duty. He was able to save me from myself. With utter relief I handed him these dreadful and beautiful impulses.

As I abided daily in his Presence, he began to immediately open up the emotional part of me. I found freedom to grieve when grief was called for. When tears came, either from joy or pain, I let them come. He undammed the blocks in me which I had so cautiously erected, and flooded me with a wholesome washing. With the opening of my emotions, which distressed friends who didn't understand, great interior harmony began to be established. All my creative instincts poured forth in writing: journals, and dramas for the sanctuary, invocations and articles, written prayers and thank you notes, books and short stories.

Moreover, I began to discover that it was he who was the source of these confusing jabs I called "awful splendor." It was his way of calling me to dance the dance, sing the song, pipe the pipe that only I could dance, sing, pipe. They were his ways of arresting my attention. They were to sensitize me, absorb me, disturb me, motivate me.

On another day, I once again took the Webster's down from its shelf and looked up the word sentiment, only to discover something beautiful:

sen-ti-ment n. 1. Feeling; sensibility; also tender susceptibility.

Tender susceptibility—of course, it described completely my experience throughout childhood. I was tenderly susceptible to life, to those stabs of joy which caused in me delight and suffering, jointly.

C. S. Lewis confirmed my experience, giving me further language for this phenomenon. In the account of his conversion, *Surprised by Joy*, he refers to:

an unsatisfied desire which is itself more desirable than any other satisfaction. I call it Joy, which is here a technical term and must be sharply distinguished both from Happiness and from Pleasure. Joy (in my sense) has indeed one characteristic, and one only, in common with them; the fact that anyone who has experienced it will want it again. Apart from that, and considered only in its quality, it might be called a particular kind of unhappiness or grief. But then it is the kind we want. I doubt whether anyone who has tasted it would ever, if both were in his power, exchange it for all the pleasures in the world. But then Joy is never in our power and pleasure often is.

Again, validation, by a spiritual giant who had gone before. As Lewis journeyed toward God, it was the eventual discovery that these moments of Joy did not spring irrationally out of himself or meaninglessly out of creation, but that they had a Source, and if they had a Source, that Source must be the Creator—this line of reasoning led him nearer to conversion.

I too have come to recognize those moments of awful splendor for what they are. They are means by which he speaks to my still tender and childlike susceptibility. He was the Magician who spun magic out of nothing, who was teaching me to be comfortable with mystery. He was the Merlin calling myself unto himself.

O dear Magic-Weaver! What a relief to place into your hands these terrifying yet glorious impulses.

III INCARNATION

His love will not fail even while He is taking us through this experience of self-crucifixion so real, so terrible, that we can express it only by crying, "My God, my God, why hast Thou forsaken me?"

—A. W. Tozer, *The Divine Conquest*

Maidservant me, Lord! Maidservant me!
Force these bound hands, bent knees,
Stripped and pilloried,
Toward the marketblock of ultimate wager.
Awl this earlobe against the doorpost,
Brand flesh, mark for all to see
That I am a handmaiden of the Lord.
Handmaiden me.

Maidservant me, Lord! Maidservant me!
Whip from me the last of insurrection,
Riot and rebellion.
Name me then new. Not Sarai or Rebekkah,
Leah or doted Rachel,
But castaway Hagar, Zilpah or Bilhah,
Life breeders.
Handmaiden me today, Lord. Handmaiden me.

ONE
FOR THE HEALING OF WOMEN

Although the phone rang often at our home, it rarely rang for me. The only person who called me regularly was my mother. Consequently, there was no need to play the little family game—You Get It This Time, I Got It Last. David usually answered the phone because it was usually for him.

After my encounter with the Holy Spirit, I had been careful not to articulate the experience to anyone but my husband. First of all, I didn't really have a language for what had happened. Time, I felt, would be the best test of the efficacy of this moment. Second, I was well aware that these effusions of the divine often leave us humans a little cockeyed. (One friend with a similar history humorously declared, "They ought to lock you up for six months!") I preferred not to give the Holy Spirit a bad name by exhibiting any unusual behavior.

"If you have it, they'll know it," my father used to insist concerning all those qualities about which we are so prone to toot our own horns. "You won't have to go around telling people; *they'll tell you*."

One of the verifications of the Spirit's work was that people did begin to tell me. Within weeks of my drastic moment with God, the phone began to ring for me. On the other end of the line were women in need, some in the deepest of distress, women with arms outstretched. Torn by violence, worn by attrition, they were turning to me for help and love. Since this had never happened before, I could only reason that something in me was drawing these people unto itself.

The ringing of my phone suddenly thrust me from that passive position so common to members of the body of Christ, into the role of an activist. I began to share in the fellowship of suffering. I was suddenly exposed to the clawing, frenzied agony of this world's despair.

My wholesome background had little prepared me for the ugly discharge many vomited forth. My lack haunted me. "I've never suffered like you," I said often, secretly wondering how my inexperience might invalidate an in-depth ministry in broken lives. If I hadn't walked where they were walking, could I possibly even walk beside them?

"But I can listen," I would continue. "And I can accept you despite your pain." My background had given me one valuable excess—acceptance. Lavish love had been the gift of both my parents and my husband. Their abundant approval was now spilled into the lives of others.

Confronted with the psychological reality of broken women (and the emotional ghastliness—I remember one who lay on the floor kicking her heels and screaming, "I hate being a woman! I hate it! I hate it!"), I was intensely aware of dimensions of living—and certain kinds of dying—of which I had been blissfully ignorant. I had never heard these cries of despair, though they surrounded me. I had not been touched by this pain, nor pinpricked nor stabbed, nor had my wounds rubbed with salt. I had chosen not to see the arms outstretched for help.

Partly, my own misogynism had prevented any deep empathy. I had categorized and catalogued women into types. I had been discriminate, partial, offended by the symptoms of distress. I had kept women from myself.

At this crucial moment, the Lord arranged for another saintly window to shine into my life. Here was a special woman who insisted I understand the fact that "it is a sin to withhold love from any human." As I listened to those who came to me with stories of woe, I realized it was absolutely true—it is sin to withhold love! Furthermore, I found that it is the withholding of love, parent from child, husband from wife, friend from friend, that causes the greatest emotional damage, that cuts with the serrated edge into the tender flesh of the subconscious. My latent malefaction began to diminish as I put a guard to check against my own unintentional errors.

Painfully, with the Spirit helping me to shove, I heaved the doors of my heart open. Creaking on its hinges, rusty and making loud moanings, it finally stood ajar. Conscientiously, I oiled it with prayer.

Gradually, supernatural gifts were freed in me for the purpose of ministry. The more I prayed and brought my life into obedience with Scripture, the more I listened in quiet to my Heavenly Tutor, the more I kept myself open to those who came to me, the more I experienced the influx of these special qualities.

In a flash of knowing, psychological insight would be given beyond anything expressed by the personality before me; here was the gift of knowledge. In prayer I would find the perfect direction for the dilemma of another's pain, counsel that was regularly beyond my own experience; here was the gift of wisdom. The ability to divide between truth and its rationalization rose like an arrow to meet the bull's eye; here was the gift of discernment.

Frankly, these gifts terrified me. I had not asked for these flashes of truth, and I was wary of my own human ego. Spiritual pride is always the opposite side of the coin of spiritual growth. I was all too aware of the penalties inherent in the flipping of that coin—the abuse of spiritual gifts, that counterfeit existence in which the Enemy delights.

Frantically, I went before my Tutor, pleading for him to deliver me from the perils of spiritual egotism, to teach me how to use these miraculous insights, how to exercise the gifts, and how to keep from imposing my vaulting id upon them.

Private tutorials were immediately arranged. The instruction was exacting, to say the least, and not at all gentle. During these briefings I learned that God's standards for righteousness were awesome. There began in me a crucifixion of the petty loves, the treasured fleshly morsels, the tidbits of errant wantonness. Quickly, I came to sympathize with Isaiah's sigh, "The hand of my God was heavy upon me..."

The back side of it, particularly, became awful in its familiarity. Quarter was allowed to others, but none to me. How often I was dragged before his face, truant again! Gripped by the scruff of my neck, I would hang, squirming and protesting, my feet dangling in midair. "I can't," I would wail. "I can't be what you want me to be. It's too hard and I'm too frail. I can't take any more of this exacting discipline!"

The reply inevitably came back the same: *You can! You can! There is nothing I want you to be that you can't be! You will become what I want you to be! You will be ALL that I want you to be!*

I who had been spanked only three times in my entire childhood was now being walloped daily. Due to my fragile susceptibility, my parenting had been assigned to those willing to give love. The time had come, however, to put away childish things. There was to be nothing in me that would be a detriment to his intended use of me. I wasn't just hard-pressed. I was mashed!—My Lord, the Masher...

All the prophets will verify my experience. Once the exchange has been made, heart and soul and body and mind given to him, he takes them as his own. This pulverizing would be unendurable were it not for the fact that from each crushing there pours a sweet ointment, an oil to anoint the wounds of others. There was also the remembrance that I had asked him to save me from my pride.

One Sunday evening we held a special meeting for people who felt like they didn't fit in at the church, calling it "A Meeting for Misfits." The most beautiful people came. Out of this discussion of needs and the exploration of how to use one's abilities grew the women's growth groups, which met for the purpose of stimulating one another to spiritual development (these were eventually to mushroom into a network of varied cells throughout the church).

For the next two years, there was scarcely a time when I wasn't involved in some kind of small interaction unit, containing four to six women, which met one night weekly for two months. The first group was a prototype of all the rest to come. In it were two women experiencing the breakup of marriage, one pulling out of deep depression, and two struggling mightily to flesh out full personality development. Needless to say, we had startling interchange!

I don't know how much I helped anyone in these protracted

times of personal sharing, but I know *I* was expanded immensely. The growth groups with their intimacy of inter-mingled lives were a laboratory for me in which I formulated all my theories of interpersonal relationships. This test, performed in the glass vials of our encounters, proved to me there wasn't anyone I couldn't care for once I heard her story. This rare microscopic scrutiny pinpointed the value of accountability, of covenanting together to hold one another responsible. This crucible of pain programmed me in the meaning of being a burden bearer.

A character in Charles Williams' novel *Descent into Hell* speaks of burden-bearing as "much more like carrying a parcel instead of someone else.... If you're still carrying yours, I'm not carrying it for you—however sympathetic I may be."

"I'm afraid, so afraid," sobbed a voice on the other end of the phone. It was a pregnant woman whose husband had abandoned her when she refused an abortion. "Can you give me your fear for tonight?" I wondered. "Let me bear it for you while you sleep. Let's pray before the Lord and tell him that you are going to release this parcel to me. You will willingly put it down, and I will willingly pick it up."

We prayed. The night passed and my frame became a subconscious temple for prayer. The phone rang again the next morning. "Guess what?" said the voice, sounding rested and in control. "It works!"

I became surrogate husband for this woman when her time came. We centered down in our minds upon the labor pain, held hands, repeated calming words, and counted breathing patterns. Ironically, the sign in the waiting room to which I withdrew after she had been wheeled from me read, "The best thing a father can do for his child is love its mother."

The birthing over, the cart bearing both mother and child was rolled into the hospital corridor where I had been asked to wait. Again, here was a baby most beautiful, and not even my own. "Why? Why?" the mother groaned in anguish, lifting herself into my arms and weeping. "Why doesn't he love me, Karen? Why? Oh, why?" It is a cry that haunts me still and one for which I had no answer. There are some pains we can help one another carry and there are others which must be borne alone.

Sacrificial love slipped out of its academic hoods and gowns

and donned dungarees, slightly grubby at the knees, worn
and bare-threaded, lacking in design of any kind. For me, it
was a timorous disrobing. No one has ever been filled with
more fear in the giving of ministry than I. On my knees,
cultivating the soil of another's inner garden, I saw slip from
me my plans, my time, the privacy of my own self, my home.

We took into our home a young woman whose last two
years had been spent in a state mental hospital. David and I
came to realize she could never fully understand God's love
until she saw it fleshed out in a Christian family. She
filled the rooms of our house with her pain. Her nights were
haunted by horror and she would stave off the dreams by
delaying sleep. Consequently, her days were topsy-turvy. It
was impossible for her to hold a nine-to-five job and become
self-sufficient when she didn't rise until noon!

One morning after an awful night, David noticed that our
housemate was again late in rising. "Where is she?" he
demanded. I noticed his ire swelling.

"She's still asleep," I replied, cautiously.

"Get her out of bed," he raged. I did.

He proceeded to lecture her on planning her own life, on
being responsible, on taking hold of circumstances. No
excuses were allowed, not physical illness, not lack of sleep
because of nightmare, not unhappiness. She was sent out to
clean the maggoty garbage cans moldering in the summer heat
and to weed the plot of yard around them. I cowered before
the impending disaster I was sure his impatience was bringing
down upon our heads.

An hour later she returned from the backyard, sweaty and
smudged, but noticeably content. "Boy!" she exclaimed.
"If they'd had work like this, I would never have stayed so
long in that mental hospital!" David's approach has a *name*; it
is certainly reality therapy!

I too ran short on patience. Inadequate, I marched
innumerable times to my bedroom, slammed the door, threw
myself on my knees, and pleaded, "God, I can't love her! It's
impossible! I'm not leaving this room until you have filled
me with your love for her." I discovered he had boundless,
infinite compassion for this, our housemate. He loved her
greatly.

I held one woman in my arms all night, held her as her

personality disintegrated before my eyes, held her tightly as her mind and her emotions slipped from my grasp, watched in horror as she thrashed into the unknown netherworld of psychological fragmentation. Finally, I came to the end of human love. At last I came to the realization that in the face of this world's need, all our abilities, unincarnated, are empty.

Today, I no longer even attempt to love. All my efforts are concentrated now in God. "Pour into me yourself. Love this being through me. Touch her, using me as an instrument. You alter this disharmony, this dissonance. Incarnate me with your life. Let it spring from me to this body of pain. Amen."

So many of these women needed desperately to be held, to be reassured by physical closeness—but I was afraid, reserved, inhibited. Studying the healing ministry of Christ, I noticed how frequently he established physical contact with those broken by disease. He *touched* the leper; he *touched* the bier of the widow's son from Nain; he *laid his hands* on the sick and healed them. Taking Jairus' daughter *by the hand* he said, "Little girl, I say to you, arise!" He *put his fingers* into the ears of the deaf man with the speech impediment; he spat and *touched* his tongue. He took the blind man *by the hand*, led him out of the village, *rubbed* the spittle mixed with clay on his eyes, and *laid hands* upon him.

Finally, I have learned to touch, to touch physically, to touch emotionally, to caress with the spirit and with the soul. I have come to believe, though too late for many, that through the laying on of hands in prayer, we can be burning bushes aflame with his grace, cleansed from human desire, holy and abandoned to him.

Today, if I touch, I do it with the thought that Christ is reaching out through me, and if I lay my hands upon their heads in prayer, and if I hold them while they weep, I do it consciously surrounding myself with his Presence so that it is his nearness they feel, not my own disabled ability.

These lessons in loving were long and hard in the learning— I fumbled and stumbled. Still unaccountably, the women came, drawn to something in me that had never before existed, something of winsomeness, something of attractiveness. *They told me what it was.*

Sensing my inadequacy, I ran to him, and he exercised me

in the discipline of the taking up of crosses. He marched
me back and forward in the matter of not withholding
myself from the looking on, the hearing of, the seeing now of
pain.

So I have become garbed in the rough-spun, durable
dungarees of love, the workaday practical housedresses worn
for painting things new, for making gardens in weedy places,
for restoring old finishes. But now I have friends who dig
beside me, spade and shovel in hand, who lift brushes to wood
surfaces, who apply acid so the good grain can show.
These are the courageous women with arms outstretched who
have returned my love with their companionship, their
cordiality, their goodwill.

"Do you remember?" one reminded me recently. "Do you
remember that you told me you would walk through all the
hells of my life with me?"

*Thank you for letting me walk with you through the dark Hades
of your past and present.* We learned together—I did not teach—
the reality of Betsy ten Boom's words echoing from the
holocaust at Ravensbruck: "There is no pit so deep that Jesus
is not deeper still." Because of our journeying together,
I have discovered there is nothing to fear. There is no place
so far, so deep, so high, so wide, but that he is not farther,
deeper, higher, wider still.

Through these who have given me their friendship, I have
come to know woman. It is a knowing *about*, but also a
knowing of acquaintance. One sat in my living room
screaming in her hysteria. One woke my neighbors at three in
the morning, preaching at the top of her lungs a remarkable,
though symptomatically frightening, sermon. One picketed
in the back of the auditorium while an exposition from
Ephesians on the woman's role was preached. One wept
gently over her daughter's waywardness. One sighed, a deep
lament for her dying marriage.

I have found women who were becoming beautiful in their
ugliness and those who were fighting the ugliness in their
beauty. I found those with the restless intellects, with
burgeoning ideas. I found women who remodeled their
own kitchens, tearing out walls and laying new floors and
putting up drywall, while being seven and a half months

pregnant. "I can't tell what I smell of," one said to me. "Sawdust or perfume!" I found women who read and spun dreams and dared to suffer and were anxious to become.

I found also the God of these women. One who is not misogynist.

"Just what you need," said someone to me. "Another friend."

Another friend? Yes, another and another. I who once had none, curiously now have multitude.

TWO
AN OATH OF FEALTY

David has often had to warn me about my "jugular vein instinct." I have an uncanny ability to go for the vulnerable spot, particularly in men, often behind the soft skirts of humor, a jab which hurts all the more because it is so unexpected.

Since man/woman relationships in our culture are often combative, probably my instinct had been finely honed by the traditions of American dating. "Karen!" my mother used to comment in dismay. "Why do you treat that young man that way?"

"Mother," I would reply, nauseously certain. "He loves it. The nastier I am, the more he likes it." My instinct told me that the unattainable was always the more desirable. To mollify her I would add, "Besides, it would be harder in the end if I was nicer to them when I don't really care for them."

Something about this approach worked. During the two and a half years before I met my husband, I dated every weekend, often running in the back door after one date and out the front with another. My heart remained my own until I chose to give it away to the man who was to become my mate.

At any rate, I had become the possessor of an intuitive presentiment of the chink in a male ego. Unconsciously, I entered into competition, parried in an unspoken battle of wills, skirmished in a warfare of dominion. The victory usually came my way because this rare ability gave me unfair advantage. I even tallied the scarred flesh which lay bloodied behind me. Unincarnated power, that not put to beneficent ends, always corrupts.

It was only natural that I should have carried some of this scrapping mentality into our marriage. For a while David came in for his unfair share, but since he has the ability to yelp "Ouch, that hurt!" and has developed some effective counter-attacks, the warring in our relationship soon came to an end.

My capacity for loyalty is one of my better virtues. Teasingly, I testify to the fact that "I have spent one half of my life waiting for David, and the other half, following him around." It's not far from the truth. To admit I had failed in steadfastness would have caused me an inestimable drop in self-esteem. Consequently, on the conscious level I have never been even mentally unfaithful to my husband.

Subliminally, however, my intersexual confrontations which oought to control and not be controlled constituted the half-sister of infidelity. It was something akin to the misplacing of affections. It was a concentration on my own power in relationship to the opposite sex that was out of line. It was certainly a withholding of love and an abuse of a sensitivity that should have been turned to healing purposes.

The Lord would have none of it. He simply was not going to allow his children to be treated in such a cavalier fashion, particularly by a person in which he, himself, domiciled. The next item on his agenda was the crucifixion of this wiggling worm in me. He was quick and brutal. Simply, he humiliated me.

I had conveyed information to someone I knew would carry it directly to the very person, a male, I knew it would hurt. It was manipulative, insidious, below board. Moreover, I had misused my instinct, thrusting in an area and in a way I had no business thrusting.

Angered, the recipient of my tidbit confronted me face to face. Ordinarily, I would have enjoyed the combat, but I was becoming extremely tender-hearted in terms of soul righteousness. He let loose an arrow that found its mark. He called me a busybody. Me. His pastor's wife. *And I knew that he was right.*

"O Lord," I pleaded. "Forgive me for the awful mess I've made."

I was not to be bailed out by simple confession springing from my wounded ego. There was a life-change to be formed in me. Now.

Even my husband, who usually can find no wrong, refused to commiserate when I told him what I'd done. "I've warned you," he reminded me. "And what's more, I think this is basically your fault. Don't you know you're giving off sexual signals. You light up when certain people enter the room."

If this was so, I hoped it was only due to the sudden smell of combat, not that safe, but despicable, form of flirtation I had noticed other married women playing.

Crushed, I nevertheless took the criticism before the Lord. "Teach me what it is you want me to know," I cried. He had me where he wanted me. I opened my Scriptures to continue my reading in Jeremiah. Certain phrases in chapter two stood out painfully for me, burning on the pages.

I remember the devotion of your youth,
your love as a bride,
how you followed me in the wilderness,
in a land not sown.

. . . For long ago you broke your yoke
and burst your bonds;
and you said, "I will not serve."
Yea, upon every high hill and under
every green tree you bowed down as a harlot.

. . . Look at your way in the valley;
know what you have done—
a restive camel interlacing her tracks,
a wild ass used to the wilderness,
in her heat sniffing the wind!
Who can restrain her lust?
None who seek her need weary themselves;
in her month they will find her.

Jer. 2:2, 20, 23, 24

My answer was graphic to say the least. This is a sample of his heavy-handed dealings with me. I, who of all women, considered myself most faithful, had a chink in my marital defenses. Though I did not allow myself to be overtly flirtatious, my subtle combat flailed away in the arena of sexual attraction. It was a crack that foretold future doom, and God would not allow it to exist in me. I was to learn that one's marital fidelity, one's sexual fidelity is *always* a symbol of the condition of one's fidelity to God.

A day later I recorded in my notebook these words from the Psalms, "Hear, O daughter, consider, and incline your ear, forget your people and your father's house and the king will desire your beauty. Since he is your lord, bow to him..."

I bowed with his heavy hand upon my head in an oath of fealty.

There is to be no more battle for dominion, I heard the voice.

"Yes, my Lord."

There is to be a truce, a laying aside of weapons.

"Yes, of course, my Lord."

From this point on there is to be utter integrity in the meeting of the sexes. You are not to use your powers in any way to draw attention to yourself.

"I understand, my Lord."

Above all, you are to use the gift of knowing of pain to heal; take no more unfair advantage in the wounding. And furthermore, if you once use it again as a power play with another male human, the blood will be upon your head. Do you understand?

"Completely, my liege."

Good.

Since then I have learned to view the opposite sex as child, son, brother, friend, fellow-worker, father, but never as combatant.

I have submitted. I have laid aside my sword.

Consequently, my faithfulness is complete, has become a circle rounded.

THREE
THE LORD HONORS THOSE...

I have never waited for any man as I waited for the postman.
The housekeeper coming three afternoons a week was like
a hungry thing, with an insatiable appetite for funds. The
postman brought me checks, payments for my free-lance
work which had been accepted.

Sixty dollars today doesn't seem like so much money, but
at that time, when I had never had any money of my own,
when the economy was not so inflated, and in the home
of a pastor, it seemed immense. I was sixty dollars in arrears
and it seemed like six hundred!

Though I had taken a huge step when I hired a helper to
aid me in my homemaking responsibilities so I would be free
to develop my writing skills, tonight my faith was wavering.
A check should have been in the mail a week ago. I couldn't
borrow the money from David. (He probably didn't have
any either.) At any rate, it would have been unfair to
shoulder him with my financial obligations, and my student
aide needed the money to help her through school.

"Lord," I had been pleading, "please let that postman
come with a check for me tomorrow." But no money came
in that day's delivery, or in the next day's or the next.

Maybe someone had pilfered the check, or perhaps it had
been lost. Worse yet, maybe the publishers had found my little
piece unacceptable and there would be a letter instead,

saying, "Thank you so much for your submission. Due to our volume of material, we are sorry to inform you..."

I had dedicated the evening to spend time in petition before my Maker.

After a prolonged period of prayer, I suddenly recalled the words I had read months before. I thought I remembered the source. They were: *The Lord always honors those who trust him*.

I was suddenly faced with a crucial question. Was he able to be trusted? I had done all that was in my human power to become the person he wanted me to be. To be able to write meant overcoming gaping pits in my natural personality, changing the course of a river in midstream, vaulting mountains. I had insured that my primary responsibilities— home and husband and children—were well cared for so I would not be debilitated by guilt and I would not be subject to criticism.

The Lord always honors those who trust him. What was that source? I searched the pages of the book where I thought I had read those words. Nothing.

The postman and my delayed checks were only a symbol of a basic decision that had to be made. Could I trust him? If so, then I wouldn't need to worry about whether that check would be in the mail tomorrow. That would be God's problem. I had done the agonizing to bring my life into as much as I knew of his will. I was writing, obedient to what I sensed were the desires of my Creator. Scared to death that no one would like my work, I was nevertheless writing and risking rejection, even working myself into a possible financial hole—but could I trust him to take care of my needs, to honor me?

Point and counterpoint, the phrases set off each other. The Lord always honors those who—but could I—trust him?

"I trust you, Lord," I whispered. "No matter what happens in these next days, whether that check comes or not, I trust you to take care of me and honor me because of my implicit regard for you."

My husband has a thing about worship. The church he started in the inner city of Chicago never experienced a Sunday while he was pastor without having its attention focused in praise of the Godhead. Each service was coordinated around a preaching theme from the Word; the proper response was determined, and then an attribute of God, or a characteristic of his nature, was chosen for adoration. As a corporate unit, we praised him for qualities I never dreamed existed. Worship was narrowly defined for purposes of clarification as "attributing worth to God."

For the first time in my life, to go to church on Sunday morning was a joy. My comprehension of the Almighty expanded marvelously and I began to be proficient at the objective detailing and expressing of what I liked about God.

This night, however, after I had breathed those simple words of trust, I did not praise. Or rather I was not the source of it. Praise poured into me. Something wonderfully warm filled my heart and I began to tell God how much I loved him, how I wanted to serve him. I opened my Bible to those last few Psalms of adoration and vaulted them past the ceiling, past the near heavens, past the universals.

I could trust him. I could trust him! He was worthy to be trusted with the whole of my being, explicitly and implicitly. Halleluia. Amen.

Sound the cymbals, blow the trumpets. Break forth into clapping. He is worthy to be trusted.

The mailman came the next day, and along with him came my check. I paid the housekeeper and she in turn went to the business department in her Bible college and we were all content.

I had learned a basic lesson, had an experience of spiritual growth incarnate, one that is supremely important when the soul is facing the dark night of crucifixion. He can be trusted, and he always honors those who trust him.

FOUR
THE POSITIVE OPPOSITE

There is a solitude of space
A solitude of sea
A solitude of death, but these
Society shall be
Compared with that profounder site
That polar privacy
A soul admitted to itself—
Finite infinity.

—Emily Dickinson, *Final Harvest*

Whereas I had filled seventeen pages of my prayer notebook in three years, after the filling of the Spirit in my life, I covered seventy-one in the following year. My hunger for communion with the One I had come to know as being there—that One who was both transcendent as well as immanent—was immense.

My prayer notebook has become a record of my journeys into "finite infinity." Years of my personal spiritual agony and ecstasy are recorded in my varied handwritings, the scrawl when I was in a hurry or in pain, the backhand slant when I was feeling renegade, the unrushed cursive with its odd breaks and dashes. Though I often felt gauche as to my spiritual condition at the time of the writing, now these jottings give me pleasure. They are the record of a soul hungry

for God. He could not possibly refuse one "so blithe to come
to him."

These are not neat and tidy pages, they are scribbled with
grocery lists and reminders to write thank-you notes and
to make phone calls. When the children needed something to
do during worship services, the pages of these notebooks were
opened to them and the illustrations which adorn my
journals of the soul are remarkable indeed; kindergarten
renditions of humans, elaborate interplanetary creatures all
three-fingered, houses with peaked roofs, a door and two
windows, smoke curling from chimneys, and identical flowers
rowed in front. I have never seen any structure like these,
but all preschoolers draw them. Perhaps the image comes to
them in their dreams.

To record the points of extreme pain in my life, there are
blanks, often indicating a gap of weeks or months. This
does not mean I cease to pray when I am suffering, only that
the communion is so unutterable that paper cannot contain it.
I can rarely write when in pain and am amazed by the
diaries of someone like Anne Morrow Lindbergh who poured
out the agony of the days following the kidnaping and death
of her firstborn son. It seems as though I can only write
about pain in retrospect.

The lessons of prayer were enormous. Looking into the
Scriptures, I perceived that fasting was an area of discipline
taken for granted in those biblical accounts. When the
disciples asked Jesus why they could not cast out the demon
in the boy whose father implored the Lord at the bottom
of the Mount of Transfiguration, Jesus replied, "This kind
cannot be driven out by anything but prayer and fasting."
It seemed obvious to me that spiritual power was related in
some way to the regular exercise of this discipline.

The first time I fasted, unusual things occurred. A black
cloud settled over me. Attending a baby shower with
church people, I looked around the room and discovered there
was not one person I regarded with favor. Slipping into
a bedroom, I prayed that the Lord would lift this puzzling,
negative mindset from me.

The gloom simply would not lift, continuing for several
days. I began to wonder what on earth was wrong with me,

as I saw no indications of instant spiritual power at work.
Opening the Scriptures, I studied the accounts of Christ's
wilderness sojourn prior to his public ministry. "And he fasted
forty days and forty nights, and afterward he was hungry.
And the tempter came and said to him . . ."
   Of course! My darkness was the handiwork of the Evil One.
   This realization became integrated one summer morning
as I was standing, rather belatedly, before the bathroom
mirror getting dressed. I remembered the verse from James,
"Resist the devil and he will flee from you." I could clearly
understand the quick, incisive thrust with the sword of the
Spirit, the Word of God, that Christ had employed against
his temptor. So I lunged. "In the name of Jesus Christ,
I resist your power in my life to bring me into blackness. Be
gone. Leave me alone."
   Within minutes, while I was still standing before the mirror,
my daughter was at my elbow. She had just returned from
an early trip to her favorite haunt, the shopping strip just a
couple of blocks from our home, a place where a child
with nickels and pennies and dimes could feel like a
millionaire. "Here, Mommy," she said. "I bought you your
favorite candy." There they were, licorice sticks, red ones,
a whole large package.
   "Hey! Hey! Hey!" called my husband's voice from
downstairs. He was returning from an early morning
counseling session. "I stopped at McDonald's and I brought
you an Egg McMuffin. Come have breakfast with me."
   But I'm fasting!—I started to say. Then it hit me. I
remembered the rest of that portion from the account of
Christ's temptation: "Then the devil left him, and behold,
angels came and ministered to him." I laughed. These were
my ministering angels, my family with their gifts of love.
I ate the Egg McMuffin first, then some candy. The gloom, of
course, was gone.
   Fasting is still a mystery to me in many ways. I only know
that I often open myself to direct spiritual confrontation
when I attempt to fast. I have come to anticipate it. It is this
regular resistance, these attempts to discourage me, that
have convinced me of the tremendous link between this form
of practiced righteousness and spiritual power.

Another prayer power I discovered was what I have come to term "prayers of the positive opposite." In the Old and New Testaments there are interwoven strands of commands which teach us to respond to the crises of life in a way radically opposed to natural human responses. They advise the exact opposite of what we normally say, feel, think, and act. The human response to crises is generally negative. These are positive and they take their best form in prayer.

"You have heard that it was said, 'You shall love your neighbor and hate your enemy.' But I say to you, Love your enemies and pray for those who persecute you..." These words of Christ are elaborated on by the Apostle Paul in Romans 12. "Bless those who persecute you; bless and do not curse them. Repay no one evil for evil, but take thought for what is noble in the sight of all. Beloved, never avenge yourself. No [and here, Paul quotes from the Old Testament], if your enemy is hungry, feed him; if he is thirsty, give him drink... Do not be overcome by evil, but overcome evil with good."

In response to Scripture I practiced an obedience without really understanding why. I began to pray for those who despitefully used me, to utter blessing into their lives, to ask that he would make their days full of joy, that he would bring them wholeness and give them material and spiritual benefits.

At the same time I was discovering the vast number of Scripture verses which insisted on praise in the crises. Ephesians 5:18: "... be filled with the Spirit... always and for everything giving thanks in the name of our Lord Jesus Christ to God the Father." Acts 5:41: "Then they left the presence of the council, rejoicing that they were counted worthy to suffer dishonor for the name." Then 1 Thessalonians 5:16-18 (TLB): "Always be joyful. Always keep on praying. No matter what happens, always be thankful, for this is God's will for you who belong to Jesus Christ. And 1 Peter 4:12: "Beloved, do not be surprised at the fiery ordeal which comes upon you to prove you, as though something strange were happening to you. But rejoice..." James 1:2: "Count it all joy, my brethren, when you meet various trials..."

The list goes on and I found that I could not ignore any

teaching of such volume. I began to praise God and thank him when I encountered difficult things.

At dusk one evening, I watched with horror as a speeding bicycle slammed into our three-year-old. I could see it coming, the child and the vehicle approaching the same point at the same time. That memory recalls my wild cry, "Oh, no! Oh, no! Oh, no!" When I pulled the little form away from the still-spinning wheels his head was covered with blood spurting from a deep gash just a fraction above his eye.

Cradling the child, my baby, in my arms, I began the prayers of rejoicing (do you see how absolutely unnatural this is?). "I praise you, Lord, that you are absolutely in control. There is nothing that escapes your sovereignty. Thank you that there are no broken bones. I praise you that you provided an angel to keep this little one from the power of death. I praise you that the gash is over the eye and not on it, that there will be full sight for him to see the days ahead. I rejoice in this incident. I will not allow it to conform me to the way of the world..."

Rushing to the emergency room, I could feel Jeremy relax in my arms. He sustained twelve stitches without a whimper, without a squirm, without one indication of fear. True, a shot of Novocain was administered, but the plastic surgeon who had been called from a party (and who still smelled of that party) pulled back the green curtain in the emergency room and looked slightly aghast. "Some kid!" he pronounced. "What are you raising in there? A stoic?"

Some might think the child was in shock. Perhaps. He certainly didn't seem to be in shock, laughing and making jokes with me about how tough he was going to look with his scar and about how he could brag to the kids on the block. Perhaps it was the natural anesthesia of the body against pain. Perhaps. But no theory will ever disprove my unfaltering belief. I was certain that the calm was unearthly, an interlude brought about by the Presence, who was free to move into our crisis because of my prayers of praise and thanks and rejoicing.

There is power in the positive opposite. When we lift our hearts in gladness at the moment of all of life's dilemmas, large or small, we have immediately removed ourselves from the encroaching dominion, the negative persuasion of this world's dark Overlord. This is the ultimate technique in spiritual warfare—to face our human inquisitor who holds over us the power of physical torment with prayers of blessing on our lips. We will be, we *are* removed from their power to hinder our souls. Imprisoned physically, we are nevertheless free!

To thank God when we are delayed in traffic testifies that we believe he is in control of the mundane. It helps us to suspect that perhaps we have been preserved from mangling on the road ahead. To praise him for pain, because it teaches us to identify with the suffering of the innocent, who pant and die and moan in the world around us, enables us to cast our prayers with their lot, frees us from the encroachment of that torture chamber upon our spirits.

All these are like cries, rallying shouts, going up from the battleplace, a banner floating in the breeze above the encamped tents of light. *He is Lord of all!* Thus we affirm our kinship to the King. He is Lord over our bodies! He is Lord over our time! Thus we affirm his ability to bring good out of anything, to redeem the unredeemable, to make new the sin-blasted old. He is Lord over our enemies! He is conqueror of all the ultimate despairs!

So I lift my heart in praise and thanksgiving over the beautiful good and the terrible bad. I pray goodness into the lives of those who are evil toward me. I am freed from being consumed by what is good because I recognize him to be the giver of it. I am released from the hold of the negative. My enemy is no longer. God has overcome evil with good.

Column X, *Manual of Discipline*, the Dead Sea Scrolls, reads:

As long as I live it shall be a rule engraved on my tongue to bring praise like fruit for an offering and my lips as a sacrificial gift. I will serve God's glory, and the flute of my lips will I raise in praise of His rule of righteousness. Both morning and evening I shall enter into the Covenant of God: and at the end of both I shall recite His commandments, and so long as they continue to exist, there will be my frontier and my journey's end.

Therefore I will bless His name in all I do, before I move hand or foot, whenever I go out or come in, when I sit down and when I rise, even when lying on my couch, I will chant His praise.

My lips shall praise Him as I sit at the table which is set for all, and before I lift my hand to partake of any nourishment from the delicious fruits of the earth.

When fear and terror come, and there is only anguish and distress, I will still bless and thank Him for His wondrous deeds, and meditate upon His power, and lean upon His mercies all day long. For I know that in His hand is justice for all that live, and all His works are true. So when trouble comes, or salvation, I praise Him just the same.

Among all these lessons of prayer was added the tremendous efficacy of the solitude of the soul. The reason our spirits are so often pygmied is that the spirit is nurtured quickest in silence. "In returning and rest you shall be saved; in quietness and trust shall be your strength," confides Isaiah.

Daily I withdrew, quieted my spirit, closed the Scriptures, and waited before the Lord. In time I began to experience the physiological benefits testified to by humanist meditationists—the calming of the nervous system, the relaxed breathing patterns, the peace—but because mine was not only a human effort but the opening of my mentality to him, the restful fixing of my mind on God and his Presence, I consequently found one day that I had entered into the reality of the Scriptures I had once found so puzzling.

"Abide in me, and I in you. As the branch cannot bear fruit by itself, unless it abides in the vine, neither can you, unless you abide in me. I am the vine, you are the branches. He who abides in me, and I in him, he it is that bears much fruit..." John 15:4, 5. "For we who have believed enter that rest... Since therefore it remains for some to enter it, and those who formerly received the good news failed to enter because of disobedience... let us therefore strive to enter that same rest, that no one fall by the same sort of disobedience" Hebrews 4:3, 6, 11.

They seemed perfectly clear. Through the regular practice of solitude before God I was entering into the rest of God, a forerunner of that final Sabbath. I was, through Scripture study, prayer, and communion, daily abiding in Christ.

My soul was being stretched. My experience was finally matching my knowledge.

FIVE
HURDLES OF EXPERIENCE

People often accused me of leaning too much to "the experiential." Perhaps these criticisms were just. Whenever we attempt to rectify a lack in our lives, we often over-compensate. Attempting to move into a knowing of God by acquaintance, perhaps I erred.

One night of despair was set off by just such a comment. Weary with over-ministry, insecure because of my forays into the subjective, I needed more than anything a pat on the head. What I received instead was a poke in the pother.

"Karen," chided my friend. "You lean too much to experience!"

Checking the retort, I thought, "And you, my dear, are afraid of experiencing God at all!" Then I heard a still, small voice which seemed to be speaking louder than my rising ire: *Submit to this exhortation. There are great lessons to be learned here.*

So I listened as my tenderest of tender points was knobbly-kneed. The criticisms were about my excesses, the fear of which had haunted my steps into spiritual growth. Yes, I all too well knew that overdependence on experience often does result in uncontrolled emotionalism. Yes, we are called to walk by faith, not by sight. Yes, our experience must always be servant to our theology. Yes. Yes.

All these years I had been deliberately struggling in the

experience of Christianity. I had been catapulted out of mere academic understanding and into acquaintance with God. Those truths from my past, those which had been either hidden or halved or fully proclaimed, but not received, began to take on reality. I had been stepping—rather, leaping— into becoming a doer of the Word.

These hurdles, often compelled by a force beyond myself, were fraught with terror. They were not altogether blind leaps, for I was vaulting in strict obedience to the objective written Scriptures and to the subjective nudging of the Spirit within. My fear sprang from the fact that I had no idea where I would land once I jumped or what condition I would be in after the leaping.

Timidly, because of my fear of what others might think about all these wild efforts, but doggedly because of my alarm about being disobedient, I plunged into experiments of faith. For instance, I saw in my study of Scripture that power for healing, both physical and emotional, was available for today. Responding to the inward prodding of the Spirit, who would not leave me alone, I began reading current literature, compiling further biblical research, attending conferences, extending my faltering self in prayers for healing.

With every new area of growth I had to walk through fear, and this was no exception. There was fear of what others would think if I visited hospital rooms and prayed for spiritual healing, fear of God withdrawing his Presence if I didn't, fear of what men would say if I, a woman, began to minister in traditionally male ways, fear that they might be correct, fear of giving love to people who had not requested love and who did not want mine. Terror was multiplied upon terror, then multiplied again by the fact that I was learning I couldn't program God. The surety of his actions was not in direct proportion to my obedience. Our timing— mine human and his infinite—were rarely in sync. His desires were often unfathomable, "his ways past finding out."

Still I leapt in one area of growth after another, gathering my skirts of insecurity in hand, swallowing the lump rising in my throat. But criticisms came; few understood what was happening, and fewer still pressed my hand as if to say, "We're glad at least that you're leaping." I often did land in marshy bogs and in tormented positions, making necessary

yet another terrible spring. This trampolining up and
down, forward and back, was stimulated not by a lust for
experience in itself, but by a desire to be able to see, hear,
smell, taste, or touch the Lord. I was desperate for more
of God.

I spent that night on my knees. Had I gone too far? Was
I becoming half-cocked? Had I become enamored with the
efforts of leaping? Was I delighting in leaping for leaping's
sake, my ego expecting the commotion to attract the attention
of my fellow humans? Was I becoming some sort of religious
neurotic?

"Lord," I prayed. "Did you bring this word of exhortation
into my life to warn me? Do you want me to stop this striving?
Have I been working against your will? Have I been speaking
or acting unseemly?"

As usual, when I wanted him to speak, he was silent.

Feeling faint flushes of humiliation, I went to bed. I was
vaguely suspicious that I had been making a fool of myself.
How could any ordinary human think to experience the
mysteries of God? Those encounters were reserved for the
sacred few, for the desert-blasted Moseses, chosen despite
their wishes. It is for these that God cracks the mountains,
enshrouded with fire and smoke, and to these only he gives
glimpses of himself.

Concluding that God had rebuked me through the words of
my friend, I slept fitfully, wrapping silky-edged shame
around me for a cover.

A bird woke me the next morning, a newday dawn bird,
trilling one clear call-note, whistling for my attention. "O
Lord," I whispered. "It is so pure, so clear-call pure."

Immediately the words came rushing into my consciousness,
perfectly quoted with a reference: "Ever since the creation
of the world his invisible nature, namely, his eternal power
and deity, has been clearly perceived in the things that have
been made. Romans 1."

Next: "The heavens are telling the glory of God, and the
firmament proclaims his handiwork. Day to day pours forth
speech, and night to night declares knowledge. Psalm 19."

A little startled, I responded, "Yes, that's right. You are
manifested in and through your creation."

*What do you say to the experience of Moses and the burning
bush?* came the still, the insistent voice.
Before I could comprehend, let alone answer, another
question tumbled forth: *What do you say to the experience of
Abraham upon Mt. Moriah?* Something began to stir within,
something was climbing to the tower of my hope.
*What about Abraham? What about Abraham meeting three holy
visitors, Abraham meeting the sacred priest Melchizedek, Abraham
leading his promised son to the altar of sacrifice? What about
all these experiences in which God was manifested?* A hand
was upon the rope in my bell tower.
I grabbed my Bible to verify the words. Abraham and Isaac;
Jacob dreaming at Haran and wrestling with God at the
ford of the Jabbok; Joseph interpreting the messages of God
through his dreams; Moses casting forth his rod and
witnessing the miracles of God through his acts; Joshua and
Gideon, flashing forth in the blaring of trumpets, the
crashing of pitchers; the kings and the prophets, visions and
visitations. The bells began to toll, single, distinct, loud calls.
What do you say, the voice went on, very indignant. *What
do you say to Christ's experience of the dove descending, of
his hunger in the wilderness of temptation, of blood-sweat dropped
in Gethsemane gardens? What do you say to the crash of the
mallet, to nail-pierced pain searingly shot? To the agony of shortened
breath? What do you say to the experience of redemption?*
Carillons began, one bell displaced by many, rising cantos of
pealing praise, wind-trilled carols.
*What do you say to the apostles? to Paul who knew a man
caught up into the third heaven, of John's experience of
visionary revelation? What do you say?*
The ringing stopped. Now there was silence, but I knew.
I knew. It was all a record of experience, a chronicle of man's
interchange with a real God, a record of mind and form
and spirit interacting in history and time. Men and women
through both testaments testify to the Supernatural inserting
itself into their natural worlds.
The word of the Lord came to prophet and priest and
ordinary person through his extraordinary experiential
revelation. God interacts with his world. Dust is formed.
Smoke covers the mountains. Fire strikes the altar. His voice

speaks. We are invited to taste his goodness, to seek him and find, not only in the academic, but in the wedding of the academic to the acquaintance, each one authenticating the other. Each moment holds the possibility of that ancient cry of Jacob: "Surely the Lord was in this place and I did not know it!" He is here, and in all the days and in all life.

The bird sang again, one clear-clean morning call. The muffled dawn, pink-streaked, rosette, rose. Another day was upon us, another new day in which to see, hear, smell, taste, and touch.

SIX
"TO KNOW HIM"

"To know him" was the chief goal of one of my New Year's resolutions. I was concerned about my vision of Christ. Whereas the nature of God the Father was becoming firmly implanted in my mind, and the personality of the Holy Spirit had become real, my image of Jesus still came very much out of Sunday school paper pictures.

"Lord," I prayed, "will you show me yourself?"

I had been reading in Isaiah and had never before noticed those words from chapter thirty which now seemed to jump from the pages. I recorded them in my notebook and took them as a Scripture promise for that new year.

And though the Lord give you the bread of adversity and the water of affliction, yet your Teacher will not hide himself any more, but your eyes shall see your Teacher. And your ears shall hear a word behind you, saying, "This is the way, walk in it," when you turn to the right or when you turn to the left (vv. 20, 21).

The first Sunday of that new year, John Stott was the guest speaker in our pulpit. His theme was the preeminence of Christ. I felt certain that Christ would allow me to "know him" that year in an unusual way.

Soon after this, someone unloaded a small round of buckshot at me. It was an unfair criticism, delivered third-hand. If there had been any truth in it, I would have tried to apply it. This salvo, however, was a complete misjudgment of my good motives. Unjust criticism always unravels me. I fell into a fit of weeping which I could not stop. Perhaps I had stored the pain from other similar comments and it was all spilling forth now. At any rate, I had one grand cry.

After a while I thought, this is silly, to be wasting all this emotional energy on something which is so petty. If I'm going to cry, why not apply my tears toward real pain? So I began to imagine all of this world's griefs and to weep for them, for the starving thousands of Gambia, Mali, and Mauritania, for the malnourished of Bangladesh, for the women raped in violent streets, for my Christian brothers rotting in prisons.

Suddenly, my imagination was enlightened. I realized I was weeping for all those things for which Christ died. Clearly, I could see the cross jutting endlessly from earth into eternity. There was a darkness surrounding it, and although I was not hanging there, I was in the mind of the person who was impaled on that cross. I was not suffering, but I was very close to the one who was. Somehow, we were lifted up, both of us suspended in time.

In writing there is a technical term for the approach the author has decided to use to tell his tale. This is called viewpoint. "Whose viewpoint are you attempting to express?" is an excellent question which often clears many a muddled narrative water. Through my tears, I suddenly was brought into the viewpoint of Christ as he was being crucified.

Before us passed a parade of all the things for which one should weep, all the ghastly, gory inhumanities. Babies with bellies bloated in starvation. Cannibalism. Slave ships with their horror of rotted flesh, putrid excrement. Fathers hating their offspring. Sexual depravity. Sadists enjoying others' pain. Wanton women. Here were all the things for which Christ was suffering. They swirled in black clouds, surrealistically, before the jutted cross.

"O Lord," I whispered, still weeping. "How could you become sin for these? How could you suffer for these?"

I suffered for you, my love, came the voice from that figure hanging on the cross. *I became sin for you. Will you suffer for me?*

I was startled. Was this my runaway imagination unhinged by emotional profligacy? Or was it a sacred moment, a mountain in my mind, cracking with illumination?

My prayer had been to know him. Paul's words came back to me, "That I might know him, and the power of his resurrection *and the fellowship of his suffering*." Not wanting to be guilty of treading leather-shod over holy ground, I cast aside my shoes. "Yes, Lord," I whispered. "I will suffer for you."

Permission was given. Privilege was granted. From that moment, he led me into a knowledge of him through the door of pain. My griefs were the ones he knew I could bear. They were not as deep as those that some have carried. They were deeper than others. It was a crucifixion that continued over two and a half years. At one point my prayer notebook records my cry, "You have broken me utterly. Break me utterly still."

First I began to experience the pain of others. I would pray for people, and their despair would become my own. I remember laying hands on someone who was emotionally unstable; I ached physically for two weeks afterwards. This happened frequently enough that I learned to discount the theory that the source of my discomfort was a low-grade virus. A scrawled series of prayers in my notebook reveals what was coming to be a frequent condition.

Under tremendous attack physically and emotionally. Thank you for some release, some sleep. I will be an instrument of your love. Now I am in need of tremendous strengthening. I implore. Give me your strength for my body. Fill me anew with your joy and love. I need help with so many things. Yard is overrun. House needs painting. Electricity is falling to pieces. I don't want to berate but I am making a fool of myself about healing. I am so tired. Completely depleted.

Unaccountably, my soul would become anguished. I learned to go to the Lord and inquire, "Whose despair am I bearing today?"

Very simply, a hedge was lifted from around us and we were buffeted. The city bent its dark shadows over our pastoral

home and its occupants became millstoned in the grinding of
its gods. Broken things came into my life, broken people,
broken dreams, broken relationships. We were an interracial
church, and I bore my share of the transferred anger
accumulated through the racism of centuries.

For years I had lived with an unstated dread. The lives of
others who suffered convinced me that a sword of Damocles
hangs above all our heads. It was only a matter of time and it
would fall on me. I was right. We each take turns walking
barefoot over the burning coals. Permission had been given.
The hedge was lifted. The pain-giver finally touched me.

My weariness eventually mastered me. I went under. There
is a blank in my prayer notebook. The last entry is a prayer of
thanks. I had prayed for a young woman in our church
who was suffering from depression. As I prayed for her a great
warmth filled my own body. I was grateful for this grace,
whatever it meant, but the handwriting is one of a person in
utter weariness.

The next entry is a month later.

*O Lord! how long since I have met w. you. Yet how near your
Presence. Thank you for the healing that is coming to my frayed
and exhausted nervous condition.*

*Praise you for breakdown, for deepening us through it, for intricate
timing, for so many hands helping. Use it to do work in our
lives and lives at church.*

Then there is another long, long gap.

I simply couldn't pray. During this time, someone said to me
(meaning to be kind) "If you had been depending on the
Lord, this wouldn't have happened." Depending upon the
Lord? If anything, I had been overdependent. I had been rising
every morning between 5:00 and 5:30 for an hour or two of
uninterrupted prayer and Scripture reading. I had been
setting aside hours each week for contemplation and training.
I had followed in painful obedience wherever he had
called me to go. It was not dependency I needed to learn, but
the meaning of his Presence *without my efforts.*

My shattered nerves wanted quiet, wanted the calm eye of
the hurricane. I longed just to draw my little children under

my wings, just to be mother and wife and self. The hood
was placed over the typewriter. I could no longer intercede
for this broken world. I had become broken as well. I had
become one of the women with arms outstretched.

We went away for several weeks and there was not one
moment when I was outside of his Presence. I might revile
myself for failing, but each morning on awakening there
was often a Scripture for my heart. "Come unto me all ye that
labor and are heavy-laden and I will give you rest." "Who
are my mother and my brothers? Here are my mother and
my brothers! Whoever does the will of God is my brother, and
sister, and mother." I was not to be chastised, but comforted.
All the spiritual struggle of the last years had brought
me to a place of heightened sensitivity before him, but now I
was to learn about him in another way. I was just to relax
and allow him to walk beside me.

It was six months before I felt strong again, before I resumed
my church responsibilities, before the plastic was taken
off the typewriter, before the prayers again resumed in the
notebook. I was a little older, a little wiser, but better. There
was no permanent damage, no need to be afraid of this
shadow lurking in all the future corners of my life. It was
simply a necessary interlude in my growth. After all, I
had given permission.

One Sunday during those six months, our church was
sharing together in Communion. I wasn't praying but just
being quiet before God. Suddenly, I knew his Presence was
there, in that auditorium! It was the same impression one
might have if someone walked into a room where you
were absorbed in your work. You wouldn't see the person, but
you would be certain he was near. I was certain that he
was standing in front of the ballroom which served as our
worship place, his hands outstretched toward us all. Opening
my eyes, I saw that the front of the hall was, of course,
bare. But it no longer mattered. I had seen his Presence
through another sense, a spiritual understanding. He was
there—". . . your eyes shall see your Teacher."

Along with each different unfolding revelation of pain, I
was confronted with the question "Can you trust him?" Some
residue of emotion, love, or joy usually vaulted me into

the reply I always gave, though not always willingly: "Yes, he is worthy to be trusted."

At one juncture, however, about a year into the journey, the cumulative effect of these days began to bear upon me with their heavy weight. I was in bed again, this time with mononucleosis, dependent upon the body of Christ again, a burden to all around me. Nothing distresses me more than fatigue. It seems that on every page of my notebook there is a plea for strength. Another blank—

The blank periods in this prayer diary are times of deepest crises. Now come I, crawling back to you—battered, bruised and shaken, and ashamed it would take so little to dismount me.

I cannot bring myself back to sweetness in you. My soul is weakened. Please lend me your hand. I desire to feed of you again. But you must do for me.

This incredible tiredness. Yet I cannot sleep. Can you lift this awful mourning, Lord? I feel as though I could cry all the time. I feel as though my heart, or my spirit was broken. Repair me, Lord. Somehow, please repair me.

My praise is barely more than mute.

I had finally come to terms with my own vulnerability. I very likely would face the untimely death of my husband. It had happened to others, why not to me? We very likely could lose a child. Others had bitten of this bitter suffering, why not us? I could be stricken with some crippling disease. This was the familiar daily menu for many, how could I expect to be exempt? The impregnable fortresses were all crumbling around me. I was naked before the firing squad. Then the question came again, "Can you really trust him?"

I struggled. Tears streamed down my cheeks. I tossed on those hot pillows. Could I trust him with my husband, my children, my body, my future? Could I trust him with this terrible new knowledge, that the Christian is not protected from suffering. Could I trust him? The words are there in a strong, firm hand.

I choose to believe in your inimitable goodness. I am a little child totally dependent on life support from my Father. Help me to bear all these dreadful incidents with grace.

*I know you will do something sweet for me in the days ahead. I am
anxious to observe your work. Forgive my dread when I consider
it may be more pain.*

I choose to believe in you and in your son and in your Holy Spirit.

I remember that moment. There wasn't a trace of positive
emotion stirring in me to bring about that obedient response.
There was no joy to wing me, no peace to assure me, no love
to call me. This was a cold, hard declaration of the will.
I affirmed, totally on the intellectual level, that he was worthy
to be trusted. I would choose to believe in him.

Paul says in Colossians 1:24: "Now I rejoice in my sufferings
for your sake, and in my flesh I complete what is lacking
in Christ's afflictions for the sake of his body." Years ago when
I first read those words, I was struck by Paul's audacity. To
complete the lack in Christ's afflictions—what an ego!

Now I understand that we are called to enter into the
suffering work of Christ as he still labors and broods over the
formation of his church in this world. Some of us are called
to suffer for him, to taste the deep dregs of this world's pain,
and for a time to be burden-bearers in that suffering.

I affirmed him in my physical disease. It was one in a series
of many aggravations, but it was not to be the last. People
were saying to me, "My word, lady. How can you possibly
take any more?" I was beginning to feel like a pariah.

Edith Hamilton has written, "Pain is the most
individualizing thing on earth. It is true that it is the greatest
common bond as well, but that realization comes only when
it is over. To suffer is to be alone. To watch another suffer
is to know the barrier that shuts each of us away by himself.
Only individuals can suffer."

That is the amazing thing about pain. One feels so alone.
Though surrounded by loving friends and family, I knew
these tortures were mine alone to feel. Yet the paradox is this:
We must enter that aloneness in order to be common. We
suffer in order to be able to say, "I understand. I have been
where you are now. I know what you are going through."

About midway in these two and a half years I finally had to
turn to the Lord and say, "I know in my head that you love me,
but I no longer *feel* your love. Can you show me in some small
way that you still care for me?" David came home that

night to tell me we had been invited to the shimmering island of Jamaica. He would teach and preach. I would recuperate. His love met me even in my darkness.

For the Christian, suffering is always an opportunity to identify deeper with Christ. Are we rejected by all we thought loved us? Then we know a little of his loss. Do we see all our dreams and hopes shattered in shards at our feet? Then we know something of his agony over the wanton insurrection against his beautiful and original designs. Is evil turned against us? Does it creep up, seeking to corrode our souls? Are we bent under the rack? Then we know a little of his manifest inquisition.

I asked to know him. I became familiar with that Man of sorrows, acquainted with grief, wounded for our transgressions, on whom was placed the chastisement of our sins.

My New Year's Scripture had been prophetic. Through the eating of adversity, through the swallowing of affliction, I had come to see who he was. I knew his Presence in a way I had never known it before. I looked at him and found his feet wet from forging the floods with me, his garments and flesh singed from my fires.

Healing takes time. My journal reads:

Without a doubt I have been derailed by this latest crisis out of a year and a half of crises. My inward harmony keeps short-circuiting. The components of my internal electricity have gone awry and I keep malfunctioning.

Outwardly this distress is not noticeable—but I know. I am wandering in some woods a little fearful of finding the main path. I suppose because it is so open on that trek, so vulnerable. If I can just hide for awhile in this leafy shelter—yet that too has its dangers. I might become permanently lost, going deeper and deeper into the forest that has no name but is only in my mind.

I am waiting for the Lord to restore or show me how to restore my internal rhythm.

But healing, when we are in the Presence of the Lord, always comes.

I feel as though I am finally recovering from a long illness. Several days ago I woke and the sky was beautiful! Some vacant hollow within had been filled with joy. The spirit was beginning to take new health.

It was comparable to those physical renewals—strength after influenza, a clear head after a cold, a strong step after the exhaustion of delivery. It has been a long illness—this disease brought on by these years of painful circumstances.

Thank you, Lord, that I have still functioned during this time of spiritual mending. Thank you that the lessons learned in pleasant days can help us operate by rote in unbearable moments.

Call me now to spend days by your side in a retreat that never ends.

I had prayed to know him, and he had shown me the crucifixion. I had become wounded, gone down into the grave. Yet the resurrection was close at hand.

Come, let us return to the Lord;
for he has torn, that he may heal us;
he has stricken, and he will bind us up.
After two days he will revive us;
on the third day he will raise us up,
that we may live before him.
Let us know, let us press on to know the Lord;
his going forth is sure as the dawn;
he will come to us as the showers,
as the spring rains that water the earth.

Hosea 6:1-3

SEVEN
"LORD, HAVE MERCY"

"Yessir, have mercy. Oh, sir, have mercy."

We were sitting in one of Chicago's largest Black congregations, our heads lowered in prayer. "Did they say, 'Sir'?" I whispered to my husband, our eyes now released by the echoed "Amen." He nodded and my glance swept the auditorium, noting the hat on every woman's head, the carefully positioned ushers beckoning with white-gloved hands, the winged flapping of a hundred paper fans, though it was cool March outside, the platform eldered in black-robed dignity. *Sir, have mercy.* I wondered at the sociological implications of that "Sir."

"Lord, have mercy," was a phrase frequently interjected by the Blacks at our own church. We depended upon them to assist us in dropping the inhibitions regarding worship from our past. They readily led the vital exchange between pulpit and audience which has become so pertinent to Black church culture. "Lord, have mercy," shouted one. It caught my attention for the first time and I assumed it was an expression common to Blacks.

One summer an Episcopalian friend of mine quoted a line from the Nicene Creed, and I was so moved by its beauty that I memorized the entire credo while driving from Chicago through Detroit, on our way to the Shakespeare Festival in Stratford, Ontario. With my husband catching much-needed

sleep in the back seat, and the countryside whizzing past,
I chanted to my heart's content those phrases of pure praise,
"God of gods, Light of lights, Very God of very God."

Attending a candlelight mass on Christmas Eve, I stood
proudly to repeat the Nicene Creed by heart, only to discover
it had been revised, and I, lately come to liturgy, was
decidedly still behind. "Lord, have mercy," the worshipers
responded. "Christ have mercy." *Kyrie eleison* read the Greek
in my prayer book. So it stretched back to the earliest days
of the church, this plea, this prayerful plea.

The following spring I concluded the first chapter of a book
which contained references to my father's family. I asked him
to review what had been written and correct any of my errors.

"Your great-grandmother was Southern to the core," he
reminisced about the woman who had raised him after his
own mother died. "She had so many typical expressions."
What were some of them? I wanted to know. "Oh," he replied,
hearing her again. "She used to say, 'Lawd, ha' mercy.' I
think I heard her say it a dozen times a day."

"Lawd, ha' mercy," that Kentucky hill-born woman used to
cry. *Lawd, ha' mercy* for the five little bodies she buried
under the soil. *Lawd, ha' mercy* for the untimely deaths of her
daughters-in-law, and for her grieving sons. *Lawd, ha' mercy*
for the hundreds of little incidents of life that reminded
one of pain and trouble.

Within weeks, my father himself was in the grip of some
aberrant disease. We, his family, watched as within a few
days' time he plunged into some unknown night of the mind.
Starting with a violent headache, it galloped toward minor
asphasia, senility, hallucinations, tremors, seizures,
unconsciousness, semi-coma.

One afternoon, one lonely, long afternoon, he folded and
unfolded his bedsheets. Aimlessly, confused, he folded them
again and again. My loving anguish demanded that I
participate, and together we matched the ends and edges,
folding covers and blankets and mats and pillow cases. In one
lucid moment, perhaps one of his very last, he looked at me
and breathed, "O Lord, have mercy. Lord, have mercy."
It startled me and I wondered, was he remembering his
grandmother's cry, or did he, bewildered and dismayed,
simply know that he needed mercy, mercy?

Intermediate care, rerun tests, doctors hunting for a diagnosis, faltering breathing and tubes and monitoring devices, a window in the wall, restraints—oh, my father, my father— Each new day was a violent torture of rapid regression. On three separate occasions we were told to expect the worst. The weeks stretched out and finally, weary of words of doom and of the brutal lashes of circumstances, in feeble love we hung our protest on the hospital door:

MEMO: to all who enter here, think LIVE.

Each of us fought death in the way we best knew—my sister in early pregnancy singing hymns through the gray afternoons, her voice trained by one of his own vocal students; my mother, faithful in attendance on this greatest of measurable stresses—he had once insisted on her life, now she insisted on his; my brother, warm in new faith, bringing like-minded friends to pray; my minister husband anointing with the oil of healing; my brother-in-law building new porch steps to replace the rickety railless ones, a task that had been put off for some convenient day in retirement.

And I—now it was my turn. Now to bend the questions of faith and healing over this drugged and helpless form. Where goes the spirit when the body is spending itself? Whence comes faith, from ourselves or from God? Lift now praise for this suffering. Lift now belief in the imperceptible perfect working of his will. Pray wordlessly as minutes stretch into unmarked hours. Now at last the words, the century-old words of every pressed heart, every burdened spirit, the words that are at last your own.

Say them over and over in pleading litany, *have mercy, have mercy*. Echo them with those under the dark shadow of oppression, *Sir, have mercy*. Chant them with the rough-clad saints in domed cathedrals, *Christe eleison, Kyrie eleison*. Cry them with your foremother planting children's lifeless bodies in the earth, in wait for resurrection: *Lawd, ha' mercy*. Whisper them now, your own, most muted cry, *mercy, mercy. Christ have mercy*.

EIGHT
PRONGS OF AWARENESS

One summer's day during this period, I stepped on the garden
rake. Four iron prongs penetrated the pad of my right foot.
Actually, I didn't step on it, but tripped onto it when my
muddy sandal folded under me.

With a sigh I separated the tool from my flesh, noted the
surge of blood, and thought, with the patience I was learning
to apply to these multiple crises, "The first rule of gardening
is: Don't leave rakes around prongs up."

"The Emergency Room," I thought. "ER." My knowledge
of hospital language came not from watching the medical soap
operas, but from experience. "Maybe this will be the only
time this summer."

I limped, bleeding, to the back door, and found that the
four-year-old had latched the chain, a recent compulsion. So I
limped, bleeding, to the front door, calling all the time
for my husband.

About halfway around the house, I remembered I was
learning the practice of praising my Lord in all things. "I
praise you for the garden rake," I intoned obediently.
"I praise you for allowing this to disrupt the order of my
gardening day. I praise you, and by this praise offer up
sacrifice of my lips. I trust you to bring beauty out of this."

My husband brought a basin to soak the mangled foot. Then
we started for ER. Somewhere in here the thought crossed my
mind: *Use this as symbolic stigmata.*

Stigmata! What does a good honest girl who was raised Conservative Baptist and is now married to an Evangelical Free Church pastor have to do with stigmata? Isn't that awfully Catholic?

The idea stuck and intrigued me. What are stigmata? I wondered as we filled out the necessary forms. Who had the stigmata? I perused the back of my mind, sitting behind a green curtain on the clean table, waiting for a doctor to look over the damage.

With the wounds cleaned, the release papers signed, and a tetanus shot administered, we returned home. My misstep had eaten up half the morning and would probably put me out of commission for the better part of a week. "The first rule of gardening is—"

Limping upstairs, I stretched out gratefully on the bed. By propping my foot on several pillows, I hoped to ease the perceptible swelling, and the now-rhythmic throbbing. Stig-ma-ta . . . stig-ma-ta . . . stig-ma-ta . . .

The Webster's was within reach. "Stigmata," it read. "Marks resembling the crucifixion wounds of Jesus, said to have appeared supernaturally on certain persons."

Christ had five wounds. I had four punctures in my foot. How tender the foot is! What pain there must have been for Christ to have that spike so violently intermingle with flesh, tearing ligament and muscle. He felt as much pain as I do— *but so much more.* What a baby I am. *Think of the palms of his hands. And the ungodly, inhuman beatings.* And then it came clearly to me—*You had an accident. He bore it willingly. He volunteered to bear as much pain as you are feeling in your foot and more, an eternity more.*

Books say that St. Francis of Assisi received the stigmata near the end of his life. I grabbed the little volume from my shelves, scooting my body on the bed, leaning forward to prevent the necessity of hobbling. I read his prayer. "Oh, my Lord Jesus Christ. I pray Thee to grant me two graces before I die. The first that I may feel in my soul and in my body so far as this may be, the pangs Thou didst bear in the hour of Thy most bitter passion . . . The second is that I may feel in my heart, so far as this may be, the exceeding love that enkindled Thee, O Son of God, willingly to endure such agony for us sinners."

What overwhelming devotion. His prayer was honored, they say. I am stumbling over four punctures in my foot, two of them superficial, yet he went "willingly to endure such agony for us sinners." Was this understanding a progression in maturity, a classic step one must take before one can really encounter the cross? Willingness was beginning to melt my heart.

In the next days my foot became infected, necessitating another trip to ER, resulting in a big booster shot of penicillin. Within a few days it was healing, and I rejoiced at the miracle God had built into the human body and at the gift of wonder drugs.

My husband and I continued with our plans for a brief vacation minus the four children, and even though I limped slowly and had to wear a shoe a size too large which didn't match my outfit, and kept wishing I could swing the injured part over the seat in front of me during the entire performance of *The Merchant of Venice*, I was still grateful.

The foot throbbed that night, after so much activity, and I propped it again while in bed. The uninterrupted seclusion was lush, and I continued my reading, St. Theresa of Avila this time. Soon after she had taken the habit of a nun, she became deathly ill with consumption. Her body shriveled to nothing. The disease and lack of exercise caused her limbs and muscles to shrink. For three months she lingered, all hope abandoned by the physicians. Finally she lay unconscious for four days and the last rites were administered. The open grave awaited her body.

Yet somehow she regained consciousness. With a tongue bitten to pieces, a throat parched from no liquids, a body coiled like a rope, she could only move one finger. Incredibly, she whispered a plea to be carried to the chapel for confession. Her body was so bruised, and she was in such pain, that they simply lifted her in her sheet and carried her into the chapel. From that moment she began to improve. For three years she was paralyzed. Then she began to crawl on her hands and knees—praising God.

"I am resigned to the will of God," she said, "even if he leaves me in this state forever." She was filled with patience and with joy.

What wonderful personalities I have chosen not to meet

because of my church background. St. Theresa came to be noted not only for her theological scholasticism but for her sense of humor. Legend has it that this sixteenth-century religious reformer stood mired in the mud on one of her journeys and cried to God: "If this is the way you treat your friends, no wonder you don't have many!"

Shifting the throbbing foot to a more comfortable height, I meditated again on the willing assumption of suffering. My heart was stirred once more in gratitude to this Lord. Somewhere from the past a preacher's voice intoned—*for you he died . . . for you he died.* Tears came to my eyes and I swallowed hard. For me he willingly assumed agony.

I returned to the writings of St. Theresa: "Once after communion, our Lord Jesus Christ appeared to me in a vision, as he is wont to do. I saw that he had on his head—instead of a crown of thorns—a crown of great splendor over the part where the wounds of that crown must have been. I began to be sorrowful to think how great the pain must have been because of those wounds. Our Lord told me not to be sad because of those wounds, but for the many wounds men inflict upon him now."

Suddenly it was real! Not just tears in the eyes, or a catch in the throat, but awful crushing, rushing reality.

The horror of men roughly manhandling my Lord. The stark obscenity of a cross projecting into his universe. I clutched at his robes as time whistled by. Rough, violent, blood-lusting hands tore him from me, a wilting daughter of Jerusalem, shock sitting on my head. If I had but been Mary that night to pour ointment over his feet. Those crushed, broken, how-beautiful-upon-the-mountains feet. A searing pain shot through my side, the memory of last spring's physical catastrophe. I wept that men should touch my Lord so. I wept.

I am beginning to understand that all of life is filled with pain. I will have pain, you will have pain. But all of life's catastrophes can be symbolic stigmata. Each pain we suffer is a possible Christlike experience. Paul bore the marks of Jesus in his body. Peter commanded us to rejoice in our sufferings. And one day each of us must touch the real-wood splintered cross.

I looked for one moment of time, caught somehow between there and now. "Be not sad because of those wounds, but for the many wounds men inflict upon me now."

Lord, I would not manhandle thee, treat thee roughly, pound stakes into thy sweet flesh. Cover me with thy blood. I will not press the thorns into that dear head, or sneer, or cause thee one moment of pain. Cover me with thy blood, thy blood.

NINE
"DON'T BE AFRAID..."

The walk in the snow would probably have turned the head of any girl sixteen going on seventeen. In itself, it was romantically-enough endowed. He had just appeared at the door that long-ago evening, an acquaintance seven years older than myself. "The snowfall is beautiful outside," he explained. "Would you like to come for a walk with me?"

Our midwestern prairie town had become a womb-world. The ordinary noises of people and machines had been embraced by the silence of large flakes floating, falling, filling the air.

A large part of the walk consisted of my hopping Indian-file behind his broad strides, several unpremeditated falls, and laughter which we snowballed into the white night. We met no one other than ourselves. Glowing windows and closed doors testified to saner individuals householding within. No tire tracks marked the streets or footprints marred the sidewalks, all of which had been freshly erased by the broad billows of chalky dust blown by some school-child wind. The quarter-hours chimed from the nearby clock tower, their melody sliding down snowslopes of sky.

He was different from the high school friends and college boys I had dated, older, more sure; and quite a variation on my Nordic ideal. I admitted partiality to the tall, blue-eyed blond. What was I to do with these black of blackest eyes, the deeper-than-brown hair, and this air of deliberate, serious determination?

Yet it was not the walk that turned my head, nor the mellow glow of streetlight, nor the two of us momentarily enjoying an empty world. It was his firm, unshakable belief in calling.

"Do you believe in being destined?" he ventured. "Do you believe that God sets some people apart to do a special work for him in this world?"

Upon returning home we shook out our heads like retriever dogs from the pond, drying them with the large towels proffered by my mother. Yet nothing would ever wipe the effects of that short journey from my heart. Here was a man who knew the meaning of calling, who had responded to God's irresistible beckoning.

"If David Mains asks me to marry him," I announced later to my startled mother, "whether I love him or not, I'll say yes."

Actually, he never did really ask. His approach was more of the "I don't want to tie you up now, you're so young, but when I ask you to marry me, which I fully intend to do, will you agree to be my wife?" variety. Yet before that could be answered, there was a finalization which had to take place in my own heart.

After all, just a few months before, this man had been a virtual stranger. I admired his many obvious credentials, the outstanding family background, his eager intellectual abilities, and that unique hunger after God, but more was unknown about him than known. A small breeze of fear blew within my soul. His deference and quiet considerations were appealing, but could they not, on the other hand, be signs of weakness?

I was afraid of his gentleness. And I, headstrong, impertinent, independent, had enough wisdom to sense I could possibly be a handful to handle. Any man I married would have to be woven of tough enough fiber to stand the attrition of my many moods. Could he be dominated by me? That would be fatal.

After several weeks of serious doubts, I attended a conference on spiritual growth. The speaker's name eludes me along with his face and subject. Certain of his words, however, reverberate even now out of the past. "Don't be afraid of gentleness," he taught. It was as though his eyes caught mine and he spoke to my dilemma, mine alone. "Gentleness is not weakness, *but strength under control.*"

Even then, young and silly as I was, as strangely profound as I was, the Word came unto me. This was my answer. My head had been turned in a seeking after the calling of God, my heart firmed by this message from the mouth of a servant. Soon I was to learn firsthand the essential streak of this man's strength. Stubborn and courageous, even driven—how many times was I to hear people comment, "Your husband is so intense!"? It has been all I could do to keep from being consumed by this strong and dominating personality.

Had I known the pain of ministry awaiting us in the days ahead, had I known the failures we would be forced to greet, would I have become party to that marriage agreement? Would I have been wiser to have turned my back on this vigorous force beneath its veneer of gentleness? No, because a voice whispered to my heart, that child-woman heart of seventeen. I heard it then. I hear it now.

"Don't be afraid..." it has called as we wandered together along the slippery edge of spiritual growth. "Don't be afraid..." it warned as we crossed arid wastes of soul-wilderness. "Don't be afraid..." it cried as we fought the rising waters of inundating opinion. "Don't be afraid..." it has whispered as we stared stark-eyed into the fiery chasm.

It is the voice of One who knows. Turn back? No. He chose the best, the most perfect place for me to hide my heart. He knows.

TEN
THE BALROG OF FAILURE

In J. R. R. Tolkien's *The Lord of the Rings* there is a terrifying passage in the first volume in which the little company of ringbearers are fleeing before a blood-lusting hoard of orcs and trolls from under the bowels of the mountain Moria. All the passages have been set on flame to prevent their escape, and the band of warriors finally comes to the Bridge of Khazad-Dûm, their last link to freedom.

Breathless, they approach this narrow span without kerb or rail which curves fifty feet before them across a black chasm toward the outer door. Suddenly, without warning, they turn to find that they are being pursued by something more dreadful than they had imagined, something dark and huge, filled with power and terror. It is the Balrog, a monster of monsters. With a rush it leaps across the fissure toward them while flames from the cavern below greet it, setting its streaming mane on fire. Smoke swirls surrealistically around its shadowy, terrible form.

Overcome, the hard-pressed heroes face this new horror. Some blind their eyes, some cry out in resignation. But Gandalf, that masterly wizard with his own awesome powers who captains the outcome of good against evil, sighs and mutters, "A Balrog. What an evil fortune! And I am already weary." He falters and leans heavily on his staff.

I feel as though we have stood at that Bridge of Khazad-Dûm and as though the Balrog has come against us.

We had many dreams for that little church we planted in the
inner city, that tiny place nestled against the underbelly
of the West-Side ghetto. One of them was to raise up an
interracial congregation, a body that would demonstrate that
the power of the Holy Spirit to unite us was stronger than
all the differences which sought to divide us.

Much of our ministry has been spent comforting and
encouraging other ministers. We soon detected that to
challenge the city is enough to raise the ire of the dark things
which dwell under this Moria. Approaching inner-city works
in the strength of one's humanity was much like throwing
soft flesh against stone. Something always splatters, not often
the stone. We knew many broken men.

After years in the city, there came a time when David
requested that I pray for him. Laying my hands on him, I
prayed over him and heard the words: *This is a soul weary unto
death.* I knew they were true. From that moment he became
my chief ministry. My prayers were for him. My insight was
for him. The love of Christ within me was for him. I would lie
beside his sleeping form at night and pray, pray for his
preservation, pray for the building up of his depleted spiritual
forces.

If I have one regret, it is this: that I didn't answer my
summons to spiritual growth sooner. I dallied so long.
Ironically, one of the reasons for my delay was that I was afraid
of what a radical spiritual encounter might do to my marriage.
Cowardly, I wanted David to duplicate whatever I might
experience. I wanted him to walk beside me, to shelter me in
the coming unknown. Finally I came to realize that this time it
was not David who was being called, it was I. God speaks
each one of our names uniquely. He knew it was essential
that I grow quickly because I was given to be David's
burden-bearer.

It was only after I had begun to grow deeply spiritually that
I realized David had been ahead of me all the time. Alone
he had led us all through the dark passages, through the
haunted corridors in order to find the way outside. Too long
he had stood alone at the Bridge of Khazad-Dûm guarding
against onslaught. Oh! the enormity of my delay, the enormity

of it! I who was to be the burden-bearer had dallied too long. Now he was weary unto death and there was the Balrog to be faced.

Most churches experience dark spiritual resistance, at least those that count for anything in this warfare between the kingdoms of evil and light. But the city churches seem to come under a cloud of doom which it is almost impossible to finger or to name. One only knows that it is there.

We eventually capitulated under the pressure. I think this was because there was not enough prayer power in our youthful congregation to prevent ruin. We folded at the point of our largest crack, that of our interracial fissure. The structure collapsed inward, pulling down upon our heads everything we held dear, the walls we had labored for years to build.

I watched my husband taste defeat, eat the sands and sharp shards of failure. The sword came against him. His utter destruction was imminent before my eyes. I knew because of my failure, because of my long delay, he was vulnerable. He had stood too much alone. He was weakened already.

Due to my intimacy with the Presence of Christ, sharpened by two years of pain, I was spiritually more sensitive than I had ever been before—perhaps ever will be again. I knew that something dark was coming up behind us. I had been fasting for two weeks. One night I awoke and it seemed as though that spiritual world which I could almost taste and touch was agog. Our human world cracked the next day. For us, it was not to be repaired.

Finally, I had come to David's side. We began to creep across the narrow span without kerb or rail, and when we were midway, David did something that amazed me. He deliberately cast himself into the flames. This was not suicidal. In biblical terms it is called submission. He submitted to the burning for the sake of our congregation, to keep it from being destroyed. It was to be his salvation.

I crept across the bridge in terror and in fear, wondering what kind of cinders would be delivered to me, the remains of my husband. Finally on the other side, my only wounds seemed to be a burning hole the size of a quarter over my stomach and below my breastplate, and a tendency to misplacement of step. Both eventually healed.

David came out almost purified. That is what fires are apt to do.

We failed. In the face of that defeat we were forced to give up our dreams, since now they lay shattered around us. Our own flaws had caused this failure, or at least they had contributed to it.

Yet on the other hand, perhaps we succeeded, too. We attempted a task few dared to even take up. We worked hard at it. We labored long with worthy companions. Perhaps we were never meant to undo in a few short years what it had taken centuries to create. Maybe we carried our rings as far as we were supposed to. I suspect someone else will build on the subterranean foundation we all laid, a building that could not be constructed without us.

At any rate, we faced the Balrog, David and I, he a weary wizard and I a come-lately Valkyrie war-maiden. We won! We had been well covered by the Word. Our obedience to it in crises kept away the orcs of ultimate disaster.

A year later, feeling that conditions had stabilized, David resigned his position as senior pastor. My journal records that event.

Our last elder meeting. We love these people, in so many ways our spiritual children, but we are anxious to be on the road again. On to more "misadventure"!

David and I both feel the great rightness about this. We have passed through the great chasm of trial by fire (the local church!) and have emerged whole, undestroyed, with the ugly gross humanities burned away.

David is wise, whole, warm with the love of God. His vision is intact. His gray hairs are most attractive. He is better at forty than he ever was at thirty. This has been a hard decade, but we have learned immensely from it.

. . . We are no longer Senior Pastor of the church we birthed, nursed, fondled, cherished, prayed over, wept over, loved. Our last Sunday was emotional. David could hardly make it through his

sermon, choking on every word, with the congregation sniffing and blowing their noses.

Somehow, by God's grace, we have walked away clean as whistles. Attitudes? Check. Love? Intact. Desire for serving God? Better than ever. Family? Loving and whole. Marriage? Brilliant. Personalities? Balanced. Reputation? Better than we deserve. God has worked his ineffable will in our lives and we have not been destroyed, but made more serviceable.

Fiery places are not so terrible after all, at least in the looking back.

ELEVEN
"HENANI"

"Henani—" It was the Sunday before our last in the church we had founded and served for ten years. The Liberated Wailing Wall, a singing group sponsored by the organization, *Jews for Jesus*, was conducting a program during our second morning service.

They sang a song entitled "Henani," explaining that this was the Hebrew word for "Here am I." It is the expression the child Samuel cried after he had heard the Lord calling his name.

The word struck a strong chord in my soul and I wrote it down, sounding it out phonetically, "Henani (hee-na-nee)."

Because the next Sunday was our last, David asked me to participate in the service by preparing a prayer of blessing and then praying it over the congregation.

I rose early that final Sunday morning. Many of my creative offerings to that congregation were penned early on the Sunday mornings they were given. This seems to always be a godly time for me.

Thinking back on our years of service, I reviewed the good and the bad times, mostly good. I thought of our corporate struggle to become all that we had been intended to be. I remembered the laughter, great waves of hilarity, and the love.

With gratitude, I thought of that unique congregation that

had given to me, their pastor's wife, the freedom to flail and strive and finally, to be. Very few churches, I knew, would have been so tolerant, but because of them I had been given the room to grow toward God.

What kind of a blessing could I leave to them?

What did I want for them to become?

Spiritual people, of course. A people practiced in godliness. A people who would cry, whenever they heard God calling their names, that Hebrew word which had moved me so last Sunday, "Henani! Here am I!"

I thought back over all my spiritual odyssey, to the painful awakenings, one by one, to the special summons, then to an incarnation of Christ in me through pain. I remembered that night when I had heard someone calling my name, when I had gone down to my husband's study hungry for God, when I had shouted with my soul, "I give you all that I am, now you give me all that you have for me."

I remembered something I had forgotten, that silly little ditty I had hummed after eternity had washed over me. How had it gone? What had it meant?

In that moment I knew. He had kept it hidden from me until this last Sunday. No wonder the word had meant so much to me. It had been the word he had planted in me. That song had been a child-song. The word is a word for child-hearts. *I had been singing "Henani"!*

"He-nani-nani-nani," I had hummed, never having heard the Hebrew for it. "Here am I," I had been singing, but knew it not until now. "Here am I."

Here was the blessing I was to leave to the church that I loved. It was a prayer for other hearts, souls, spirits, minds to all utter that irrevocable response, "Here are we, God! Here are we!"

So this is what he is creating in me. This is what his Word is forming in me. This is his breath breathing into me, blowing life into my soul. These are his hands laboring in my heart. I am becoming a *henani*.

Out of the gossamer chemises, into the sackcloth; out of the slippery satins and into the dunned cassocks—my habiliment has become camel's hair, leather girdled at the waist.

Mine are the vestments of the sand-blown pilgrim wending his way in an endless journey to God. My sandals have been loosened; unshod I tread across the stony pathway. Wild-eyed am I, but sane. I have seen a shadow of him, a flash of his features. Stark am I becoming, stripped of soul, wind-blasted, crying endlessly, "Here am I."

183

EPILOGUE

Last night, my father wandered away from the nursing home where he lives. Stricken, I related this incident to my teenager: "Papa ran away today..." and he laughed! And I who had so recently been in anguish due to my father's condition suddenly broke into hilarity myself. One might think it unseemly to laugh in the face of such pain—unless you had known my father. He caused us to laugh in the face of so many of life's disappointments, particularly to laugh at ourselves.

This life drama with its tearing between the twin catharsis of tragedy and laughter has played itself out, often touched by an air of unreality, ever since my father's facile mind was destroyed by encephalitis, an infection which invades the tissues of the brain, often causing coma while it accomplishes its dark tasks, a true villain of the cerebral corridors.

Our grief seems a daily one to bear; I still am tripped by tears after spending time with my father, and I wonder if it is inordinate, this being so often at cross-swords with pain. Yet, I think we mourn untimely because Daddy's condition is unnatural. There is no death here with which one can come to eventual terms. No, nor a living either, but a strange nether-world which haunts us with its inexplicable wherefores.

"My husband is buried in a cemetery," explained a compassionate friend to my mother. Both are members of a new sub-society, women without men, wearing unseen weeds that bear a strange stigma just the same. "But yours is buried in the nursing home." She is right. This is a deathly kind of living, this hovering continually between the "neither-nors." Mother is neither married nor a widow. I am neither orphaned nor a daughter. Daddy is—and he isn't.

For our family, "brain damage" can be translated: the sudden regression of a brilliant mind to vegetable state with a painfully slow restoration of some of the ordinary functions to a lifelike condition. The question, "How is your father?" evokes in me a strange helplessness. How can I say, "He lifted his fork to his mouth today," or "I think he recognizes me," or "He laughed with the grandchildren," and possibly convey the heights and depths plummeted and plunged by these simple acts?

Today, Daddy is mobile—but often feeble. His once brisk step falters and we are continually wary of falls. A gentleman still, he insists upon holding doors, and mother and I pass through them, torn between preserving his pride or preserving his balance. His judgment is impaired. The right side of his body has been more damaged than the left, and since he is right-handed, meals are often a painful if not repugnant experience for the observer. His memory and recall are aimless wanderers, leaving him on certain days more in our world, and on other days more in a vague land of his own.

The greatest difficulty, however, is with his speech. Daddy has aphasia. Aphasia is a disturbance in language function following injury to the brain. Those once highly developed verbal skills have now been reduced to a meaningless gibberish which rarely means anything to those of us who hear him, and well we wonder if it means anything to him. He responds to simple commands—"Sit here, Daddy. Put it down"—and seems to listen to explanations, but how much he comprehends is an unknown.

In his book, *The Shattered Mind*, Howard Gardner writes about aphasia:

One might suppose quite reasonably that the most complex linguistic functions—reading technical texts or understanding long sentences—would be the first to disappear, while such

relatively "primitive" capacities as repetition or the following of
commands might be spared.

What actually happens in aphasia, however, is far more
complicated . . . The relationship between such capacities as reading,
writing, naming, repeating, understanding sentences,
understanding commands, spelling, and calculating is exceedingly
intricate; almost any of them can be destroyed or spared in relative
isolation from the others, or various pairs may appear or disappear
together.

The issues raised by aphasia are mysterious and fascinating . . .

In other words, with aphasia one might be able to write, but
not read what he has written. He might be able to tally a
series of numbers, but not be able to name them. When my
father, after days of muttering, suddenly emits a sentence,
clear and lucid, entirely appropriate to the circumstances, or
when he carries the melody line of an old, familiar hymn, I am
convinced that the issues raised by the breakdown in language
are mysterious and fascinating.

I have another Father whose language many of us have
difficulty in understanding, but in this case, it is not he who
is the aphasiac. It is ourselves who have difficulty in sorting
the signals. It is the church, corporately, which is suffering
from the disabilities caused by a breakdown in language
functions.

I am intrigued by the choice of the Apostle John to describe
Christ—"In the beginning was the *Word*, and the *Word* was
with God, and the *Word* was God." Why this noun? Why not
some other? As a writer, a person to whom words are
important, essential, I have memorized these phrases, and I
roll them over and over in the pondering part of me, that
part which contemplates mystery.

"In the beginning"—that beginning is recorded in the first
chapter of Genesis, where my Bible notes the words, "And
God said," nine times. There is another rhythm that
tympanies through the Old Testament. It is the rhythm of the
phrase, "And the word of the Lord came unto . . . the word
of the Lord came unto . . ." The word of the Lord came with
burning bush and fire on the mountain and in the whirlwind.
Those to whom it came knew they had experienced that

word, and they were each irrevocably altered because of it. Yet, how did they know for sure a supernatural word had come unto them? How did they experience it? How did the child Samuel know he wasn't having a vivid nightmare? How did prophets know a vision was God-sent, and not just runaway imagination? How did the children of Israel know the shaking mountain was the power of Yahweh, and not simply volcanic eruptions? How did they know?

John undeniably believed that God was a communicative being—the Word was God. You can find cross-references to this passage in the records of God's creative acts in other parts of the Bible. John echoed a theme which is found in the ancient writs and was seemingly understood in his time as normal—when the Word of the Lord came unto us. "And the Word became flesh and dwelt among us, full of grace and truth; we have beheld his glory, glory as of the only Son from the Father."

Yet the twentieth-century church, this child of the media-crazed Now, is glutted with newspapers and magazines and junk mail. Our televisions beam images via remarkable satellite communication systems, our FM and AM and CB radio frequencies fill our hearing. Still, *we* are experiencing a vast language dysfunction, a ghastly impairment of the language of the spirit. We are hopelessly inept at hearing the One who *says*, at knowing when the Word of the Lord comes.

Shrugging our shoulders and attempting to explain away the great void, we rationalize, "But God doesn't communicate today the way he did in the Old Testament." *Aren't we really saying, "My Father is a hopeless aphasiac? He speaks in a gibberish we are helpless to understand. He is undecipherable."*

Shouldn't we rather be bringing ourselves for examination? Some hemisphere within us that controls the reception and understanding of spiritual messages has become stunted, damaged by a viral-like thing that eats away at the cells and destroys our capacities to hear and comprehend and, in turn, communicate. Perhaps we should assume that the Word of the Lord still comes, that he is the same today as he was in the beginning, One who speaks plainly and with splendor. Perhaps we should assume that he has not changed, but that it is ourselves who have developed grotesque deformities.

The hardest thing of all for my family to bear in regard to my father's condition is this absence of language. Mother is a poet, I am a writer, there are three ministers and two teachers among us—but Daddy, in some ways, was the best verbalist of us all. Family dinners were often family debates, with ideas served along with the main course, and my father always acting as devil's advocate on issues ranging from religion to politics to sociology. It was as important to think as it was important to eat.

Daddy used words well, succinctly and with emotion. He flowered them and fervored them. He inundated us with argument. I can frequently remember one of us protesting, "Now just a minute! I haven't been able to get *my* thoughts in here!"

Daddy had a gauntlet he tossed in the middle of hot debate, while issues flew. "You see what I mean?" he would insist, frequently punctuating his points with this phrase. "You see what I mean!" he would repeat, pinioning you with a direct, unwavering look that probed into your innermost heart, soul, and mind.

"You see what I mean," my husband and I would tease, inserting the well-worn phrase between every third word. What I would give to hear that beleaguered expression slip out now, fall between the incoherent ramblings, a challenge again, a weathervane of rising mental temperatures, a gun at the beginning of a verbal race to see who could build the most logical and consistent argument the fastest.

My father's words of laughter filled our lives. He was a storyteller who appreciated human foibles, enjoying his own as much as anyone else's. Eccentricities were to be savored—such as the time he went to work wearing a pair of new shoes. It rained, and he passed the day agonizing over the assumption that they had shrunk in the wetness, only to discover upon going to bed that he had worn them all that time with a stocking stuffed into each toe. Delighted when he recognized any wit on our part, he often encouraged the degeneration of family gatherings into hilarious repartee.

Daddy also freely gave away his words of love; they spilled forth in an amazing variety of expressions—crazy chortles to the newest infant, wild wrestling matches which we dubbed "ruffling," a remarkable series of tales about a homemade monster of his own invention, the Iskerry-Oskerry. "I haven't seen your kids for a week," he would chide, and off they would go, tagging after Papa, for long afternoons. He would hitch the rusty red wagon for bouncing journeys behind the tractor or for marvelous adventures on the muddy island in the creek, with him the biggest pirate of them all.

His approval extended to what we did—"You made me so proud"; to the way we looked—"Now Sweet, I've looked everyone over and without a doubt, you're the prettiest here"; as well as to who we were—"Mother and I are awfully glad you decided to come along with us." I grew up familiar with the words of love.

Is it any wonder that what *is* constantly bumps against what *was*?

The same is true of our relationship with our Father God— what is often bumps against what was. Each of us can recall experiences of former intense intimacy, when we heard him say, "I love you"; when he forced upon us a new idea, when he made us laugh. Now, for some reason, the signals are all crossed, silence is dominant, we do not know how to interpret the faint messages we do hear. We are lonely in this communicative vacuum, in this breakdown of language.

Corporately, the church also holds a mass memory of times when his Presence and the power of it have consumed our earthly places: when Solomon had finished erecting and sanctifying the Temple and it was suddenly filled with his glory, when rooms were shaken and the rush of the mighty wind of his Spirit could be heard, when revival fires blazed leaping in spontaneous combustions through the lands. If we will admit it, we are hungry for that startling knowledge of him in these days—for fire to fall on altars, for walls to tumble, for rivers to cease surging in their channels.

Generally we become hungry for the supernatural when we reach the end of ourselves—of our confining and inadequate humanity. Every so often I will return home after a social evening and sigh, "I talk too much. And what's more, I don't have a thing to say." Perhaps I have come of age. Human words, my own included, often weary me. They are often empty, or excessive. They wound carelessly. They are

pompous, depressing, exasperating, or selfish. Human words
are not enough.

I am starving for something other than the human
word, hungering after another kind of word that comes. I
have a soulish longing for the Word of the Lord. I want
the burning bushes, the fire on the mountains, the whirlwind
words. I want to hear and understand, I want to know I
have been irrevocably altered because the godly Word has
come unto me.

John describes the incarnation this way: "the Word became
flesh, dwelling among us, full of grace and truth." Let us be
careful not to limit that mysterious joining of divine with
human to an infant wailing piteously on the straw. Let us
struggle to understand that the Word becomes flesh in all of
us who believe. It dwells among us, tabernacled within us.
God incarnates us with the nativity of himself. We are born
again as his Spirit births within. This is the reality of
incarnation, this mystery of being en-godded, the human
joined with the spiritual. Now it too is full of grace and truth—
incarnation occurs over and over again.

We must force our feeble human perceptions to understand
that the Word still comes. God still speaks. He "comes unto"
us, our day, our times, our places. It is not he who is the
aphasiac. It is not his muteness which causes the breakdown
of language between Creator and creature. It is our deafness
that is responsible, our inattentiveness, our deliberate
rebellion of holding our fingers in our ears.

God is not silent. He never has been. He will never be. It
is we who have "ears to hear but do not hear." It is our
disability that prevents discourse, our very own.

Elizabeth Barrett Browning has written these words:

Earth's crammed with heaven,
And every common bush afire
* with God;*
And only he who sees takes off
* his shoes,*
The rest sit round it and pluck
* blackberries.*

(Aurora Leigh)

Exodus tells us about Moses, "And he looked, and lo, the bush was burning, yet it was not consumed. And Moses said, 'I will turn aside to see this great sight, why the bush is not burnt.' When the Lord saw that he turned aside to see, God called to him out of the bush, 'Moses, Moses!' "

The Scriptures say, *"he turned aside to see"*; it is interesting to note that God revealed himself *after* Moses had paused to investigate. It was only after he had stopped that he heard God calling his name. How many times has the common bush beside me been aflame with God? How many times have I sat around it plucking blackberries? How many times have I not turned aside to see and therefore missed the sound of God filling my ears, calling my name?

Daddy always broadened my name to its Swedish form, Kah-ren. "Kah-ren Sue," he would say. Since his illness, he has never mentioned it again, and I suppose that in the memory parts of his mind that have been destroyed, my name has been erased.

Thomas Merton, the contemplative priest said, "God utters me like a word containing a partial thought of Himself." How good to know that there is One who is always able to call our names. He calls, Father to child, and it is our part to learn what he is uttering and forming and creating in our lives. We need to set ourselves aside so we can see and hear and know, to pause to discover what of his word is becoming incarnate in us.

So now my earthly father seems to be suspended in a premature senility from which there is no escape, a state which I know would have been abhorrent to him, could he have foreseen it. We who love him shift continually through the moving sands of despair and delight, sifted by windy circumstances.

Yet I have never wished for death; though that would be an easy wish. I opt for life. A death-wish would be defiance in the face of this heavy and terrible beauty, this bitter but good gift. For Daddy has become to me a living metaphor through which I am learning about the terrors of the denial of language, the distress that comes from the breakdown of communication. Though brain-damaged, he who through life was ever a professor, is mentor to me still.

In his incapacity, he is tutoring me in graduate courses of higher and deeper learning. Poignantly, I am discovering the meaning and great value of words, and I am exploring the desperate vacuums created when there is a lack of them. I am learning from this man without a language about One who holds language, all of it, within his grasp. And as I roll those Scriptures over and over in the pondering part of me, I glimpse some of the reasons why the apostle chose to describe Christ as "the Word," and how all of Scripture is embodied in this phrase, and how it comes unto our day.

Your lack, dear father, is teaching me about the One in whom nothing is lacking. In you I find glimpses of him. Live on.

P 61, 62, 87, 102 118 a prayer. 146 Scripture quotations
SATAN LV H5